SHAREPOINT ONLINE

EXERCISES

PETER KALMSTRÖM

SHAREPOINT ONLINE EXERCISES

Welcome to *SharePoint Online Exercises*! In this book, I have gathered some exercises I have used in courses, organized by the Swedish educational company Addskills Cornerstone Group AB. The students were administrators, content creators and other SharePoint power users, so they already knew the basics of SharePoint. Now they wanted to learn how to create customized apps for their organizations.

By working with these exercises, my students learned to create common business solutions, and in the process they practised a lot of things that are useful to manage in SharePoint. I hope that you too will find my exercises helpful!

I recommend that you use *SharePoint Online Exercises* in combination with my book *SharePoint Online from Scratch*, for a more comprehensive learning. However, *SharePoint Online Exercises* can also be used independently or with other teaching materials.

In the first chapter of the book, we create an intranet with three subsites for a small business. In the continuation we will then enhance that intranet with various apps and solutions.

SharePoint Online Exercises requires no knowledge of how to write code. Microsoft has developed SharePoint so that it is possible to get substantial benefit from the platform without any coding experience. In one of the exercises I give a piece of code to insert in an .html page, but you don't have to write any code yourself to succeed with the exercises.

The demo links in this book refer to articles in the kalmstrom.com Tips section. Here you can watch video demonstrations on exercises similar to the ones I describe here.

To save space, some of the many screenshots in *SharePoint Online Exercises* has been cut where SharePoint only shows blank areas.

When this is written SharePoint Online has two interface types: the new experience and the classic experience. The new experience is focused on user friendliness and the interface is easy to use, but the classic interface gives more customization possibilities. Therefore I have most often used the classic experience in this book, even if I have made use of the new experience when possible.

SharePoint Online is an ever changing platform, so some things will change and no longer work as described in *SharePoint Online Exercises*. Therefore I recommend you to not learn by heart how to do things step by step, but instead see your work with the exercises as a way to understand SharePoint better.

Good luck with your studies!

Peter Kalmström

TABLE OF CONTENTS

CREATE A SHAREPOINT INTRANET

In our first exercise we will create a SharePoint intranet for a small company in the form of a site collection with three subsites. The sites will have a common navigation bar, but each site will have its own theme and its own apps where team members are able to share documents, photos, events and tasks. Each subsite will also have three site pages. We will use wiki links to create these pages.

To make the work efficient, we will only build one of the subsites from scratch. Then we will create a site template from that subsite and create the other two from that template. Finally we will add a video to one of the home pages.

Goal

Create a SharePoint Online intranet for a small company.

Actions

- Start with a blank site-collection.
- The company has 3 departments: Sales, Production and Support. Each of these departments should have their own subsite, where team members should be able to share

  o Documents
  o Events

- o   Tasks
- o   Photos
- A Documents library is created automatically when you create a subsite, but you have to create apps for the other shared content. Add the apps to the Quick Launch and enable Versioning for all four of them.
- As the departments collaborate a lot over boundaries, the whole intranet should share a common navigation.
- Each department area should contain 3 pages: Progress, Problems and Plans, where users can describe the current overall status of the department. These pages should be created with wiki links.
- Each department area should have its own theme.
- Choose a YouTube video and insert it into the home page of the Sales department subsite.
- Add a link that opens in a new window in the top navigation.

Demo:

http://www.kalmstrom.com/Tips/SharePoint-Online-Exercises/SharePoint-Online-Intranet.htm

➢ **Step 1, create a new site collection**

1.   Go to Office.com and click on the Admin tile.

2.   Select the SharePoint Admin center.

3.   Click on the 'New' button under the 'Site Collections' tab and select 'Private Site Collection'.

Site Collections

New Delete Propert

Private Site Collection

4. Fill out the form.

   a. Enter the Title "Company intranet".

new site collection

Title	Company Intranet
Web Site Address	https://kdemo12.sharepoint.com
	/sites/ ci

Template Selection

2013 experience version will be used

Select a language:

English

Select a template:

Collaboration Enterprise Publishing Custom

Team Site
Blog
Developer Site
Project Site
Community Site

   b. Enter the URL"ci".

   c. Select a language.

   d. Select the Team Site template.

   e. Select the Time Zone.

   f. Assign yourself as an administrator.

   g. Click OK.

➢ **Step 2, create a Sales subsite**

1. Click on 'Site Contents' in the Quick Launch.

Home

Notebook

Documents

Pages

Site contents

2. Click on '+ New' and select 'Subsite'.

+ New ⌄

List

Page

Document library

App

Subsite

3. Fill out the form:

Site contents › New SharePoint Site

Home
Notebook
Documents
Site contents
Recycle Bin

/ EDIT LINKS

Title and Description

Title:
Sales
Description:

Web Site Address

URL name:
https://kdemo12.sharepoint.com/ sales

Template Selection

Select a language:
English

Select a template:
Collaboration | Enterprise   Duet Enterprise
Team Site
Blog

a. Enter the Title "Sales".
b. Enter the URL "sales".

    c.   Select a language.

    d.   Select the Team Site template.

    e.   Select the 'Yes' radio button for 'Display this site on the top link bar of the parent site'.

Navigation Inheritance   Use the top link bar from the parent site?

        ⦿ Yes   ○ No

    f.   Click on 'Create'.

➢ **Step 3, create apps in the Sales site**

  1. Create an **Events** app.

    a.   Go to the Site Contents.

    b.   Click on New and select App.

+ New ∨

List

Page

Document library

App

Subsite

    c.   Search for 'Calendar'.

    d.   Select the Calendar app.

Calendar

    e.   Give the name "Events" to the app.

Adding Calendar   ×

Pick a name   Name:
You can add this app multiple times to your site. Give it a | Events   × |
unique name.

Advanced Options   [Create]   [Cancel]

f. Click on the 'Create' button.

2. Add the Events app to the **Quick Launch** bar.

   a. In the Site Contents, click on the ellipsis at the Events app
       and select Settings.

   | 🗓 Events | ···   Events list |
   | 🗔 MicroFeed | Settings |

   b. Click on the link 'List name, description and navigation'
       under General Settings.

   General Settings

   ▫ List name, description and navigation

   ▫ Versioning settings

   c. Select Yes for "Display this list on the Quick Launch?".

   ▮▦ Display this document library on the Quick Launch?

   ⦿ Yes   ○ No

   d. Click on Save.

3. Enable **Versioning** in the Events app.

   a. Click on the link 'Versioning settings' under General Settings.

   b. Select Yes for 'Create a version each time you edit an item in
       this list?'.

Create a version each time you edit an item in this list?

◉ Yes　○ No

Optionally limit the number of versions to retain:

☐ Keep the following number of versions:

[　　　　　]

▢ Keep drafts for the following number of approved versions:

  c.　Click OK.

4.　Create a **Tasks** app:

  a.　Go to the Site Contents.

  b.　Click on New and select App.

  c.　Search for "Tasks".

  d.　Select the Tasks app.

Tasks

  e.　Give the name "Tasks" to the app.

  f.　Click on the Create button.

5.　Add the Tasks app to the Quick Launch bar

  a.　In the Site Contents, click on the ellipsis at the Tasks app and select 'Settings'.

  b.　Click on the link 'List name, description and navigation' under General Settings.

  c.　Select Yes for 'Display this list on the Quick Launch?'.

  d.　Click on Save.

6.　Enable Versioning in the Tasks app.

  a.　Click on the link 'Versioning settings' under General Settings.

  b.　Select Yes for 'Create a version each time you edit an item in this list?'.

  c.　Click OK.

7.　Create a **Photos** app

a. Go to the Site Contents.

b. Click on New and select App.

c. Search for "pictures".

d. Select the Picture library app.

Picture Library

e. Give the name "Photos" to the app.

f. Click on the Create button.

8. Add the Photos app to the Quick Launch.

a. Open the Photos app.

b. Select the Library tab.

c. Click on the Library Settings button.

d. Click on the link 'List name, description and navigation' under General Settings.

e. Select Yes for 'Display this list on the Quick Launch?'.

f. Click on Save.

9. Enable Versioning in the Photos app.

a. Click on the link 'Versioning settings' under General Settings.

b. Select 'Create major versions' for 'Create a version each time you edit a file in this picture library?'.

c. Click OK.

➤ **Step 4, create wiki pages**

1. **Remove** the default **'Get started'** content from the Sales subsite homepage

a. Go to the Sales subsite.

b. Click on 'REMOVE THIS'.

Get started with your site REMOVE THIS

2. Create **wiki links** on the Sales site

   a. Click on the 'EDIT' link in the top right corner.

   ☆ FOLLOW ✏ EDIT ⌐⌐

   b. Write wiki links to three pages: [[Progress]] [[Problems]] [[Plans]].

   c. Click on the 'Save' at the left in the ribbon.

BROWSE	PAGE	FORMAT TEXT	INSERT

Save Check Out Paste ✂ Cut ▤ Copy ↶ Undo

Body ▼ 13px ▼

B *I* U abc x₂ x² ✏ ▾ A ▾ ✎

Edit | Clipboard | Font

Home

Documents

Recent

Appointments

Tasks

[[Progress]]

[[Problem]]

[[Plans]]

3. Create a **Progress** page

   a. Click on the wiki link 'Progress'.

   b. Click on 'Create' when asked if you want to create the page.

Progress

Problems

Plans

Newsfeed

Start a conversation

It's pretty quiet h...

Add a page ×

The page 'Progress' does not exist. Do you want to create it?

Find it at https://cornerstonesp2013jan2813.sharepoint.com/sites/PeterTest1/Sales/SitePages/Progress.aspx

[Create] [Cancel]

 c. Write the name "Progress" on the page.

 d. Add formatting to the Progress heading by clicking a Styles button.

| BROWSE | PAGE | FORMAT TEXT | INSERT |

Save Check Out Paste   Heading 1.46er B *I* U abc x₂ x² A   AaBbCcDdE AaBb AaBbCc AaBbCcDc

Edit Clipboard   Font   Paragraph   Paragraph Heading 1 Heading 2 Heading 3 Styles

Home

Documents

Recent

Appointments

Tasks

Progress

 e. Click on 'Save' in the top right corner of the page.

☆ FOLLOW   📑 SAVE   ⧉

4. Create a **Problems** page

 a. Click on the link 'Problems'.

 b. Click on 'Create' when asked if you want to create the page.

 c. Write the name "Problems" on the page.

 d. Add formatting to the Problems heading by clicking on a Styles button.

 e. Click on 'Save'.

5. Create a **Plans** page

 a. Click on the link 'Plans'.

 b. Click on 'Create' when asked if you want to create the page.

 c. Write the name "Plans" on the page.

 d. Add formatting to the Plans heading by clicking a Styles button.

 e. Click on 'Save'.

6. Check that the three pages have been created by going into Site Contents and opening the Site pages library.

➤ **Step 5, save the Sales subsite as a template**

1. Open the home page of the Sales subsite.

2. Click on the settings gear at the top of the page and select 'Site settings'.

🔔   ⚙

Office 365 settings

SharePoint settings

Add a page

Add an app

Site contents

List settings

Site settings   👆

Getting started

3. In the Site settings, click on 'Save site as template' under Site Actions.

Site Actions
Manage site features
Save site as template
Enable search configuration export
Reset to site definition
Delete this site

4. Enter the file name "Department site".

5. Enter the template name "Department site".

6. Enable 'Include Content', so that the three pages will be included in the template.

Site Settings › Save as Template ⓘ

File Name

Enter the name for this template file.

File name:

Department site

Name and Description

The name and description of this template will be displayed on the Web site template picker page when users create new Web sites.

Template name:

Department site

Template description:

Include Content

Include content in your template if you want new Web sites created from this template to include the contents of all lists and document libraries in this Web site. Some customizations, such as custom workflows, are present in the template only if you choose to include content. Including content can increase the size of your template.

Caution: Item security is not maintained in a template. If you have private content in this Web site, enabling this option is not recommended.

☑ Include Content

OK   Cancel

7. Click OK.

8. Click OK to the message.

› Operation Completed Successfully

The template has successfully been saved to the list template gallery. You can now create lists based on this template.

To manage templates in the gallery, go to the list template gallery.

To return to the list customization page, click **OK**.

OK

➢ **Step 6, create two more subsites from the Department Site template**

1. The Production site

    a. Go to the root site of the site collection.

    b. Open the Site Contents.

    c. Click on '+ New' and select 'Subsite'.

    d. Enter the title "Production" for the subsite.

    e. Enter the URL name "production".

    f. Open the 'Custom' template tab.

18

Select a template:

g. Select the "Department site" template.

h. Select Yes for 'Use the top link bar from the parent site'.

i. Click on 'Create'.

2. The **Support** site

a. Go to the Home site.

b. Open the Site contents.

c. Click on '+ New' and select 'Subsite'.

d. Enter the title "Support" for the subsite.

e. Enter the URL name "support".

f. Open the 'Custom' template tab.

g. Select the "Department site" template.

h. Select Yes for 'Use the top link bar from the parent site'.

i. Click on Create.

➢ **Step 7, set different themes for the three subsites**

1. Set a theme for the **Support** subsite.

a. Click on the settings icon at the top of the Support homepage and select 'Change the look'.

b.   Select one of the themes that has a Quick Launch.

c.   Click on 'Try' it out.

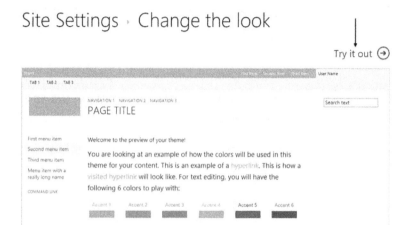

Site Settings › Change the look

Try it out →

d.   Click on Yes to keep the theme (or go back and change).

⊙ No, not quite there   Yes, keep it →

2.   Set a theme for the **Production** subsite.

   a.   Click on the settings icon at the top of the Production homepage and select 'Change the look'.

   b.   Select one of the themes that has a Quick Launch.

   c.   Click on 'Try it out'.

   d.   Click on Yes to keep the theme (or go back and change).

3.   Set a theme for the **Sales** subsite.

   a.   Click on the settings icon at the top of the Sales hóme page and select 'Change the look'.

   b.   Select one of the themes that has a Quick Launch.

   c.   Click on Try it out.

   d.   Click on Yes to keep the theme (or go back and change).

➢   **Step 8, insert a YouTube video in the homepage of the Sales subsite**

1.   Open the Sales home page.

2.   Click on the 'Edit' link in the top right corner.

3. Put the mouse cursor in an area of the page where the video should be inserted.

4. Open the 'INSERT' tab.

5. Click on 'Video and Audio'.

6. Select 'Embed' to open the Embed text box.

7. Get the applicable URL.

   a. Go to www.youtube.com and select a video to embed.

   b. Click on the video or on the title.

   c. Click on Share.

   d. Click on Embed.

   e. Change the settings for size and show options if needed.

   f. Copy the embed link.

Introduction to Kanban Task Manager for SharePoint

8. Paste the copied embed link in the SharePoint Embed text box.

9. Click on 'Insert'.

10. Save the page.

> **Step 9, top navigation link that opens in a new window**

(only for Office 365 E3 and E5 subscriptions)

1. Go to the site collection home page.

2. Activate SharePoint Server Publishing Infrastructure.

a. Click on the settings icon at the top of the page and select 'Site settings'.

b. Click on 'Site collection features' under Site Collection Administration.

Site Collection Administration
Recycle bin
Search Result Sources
Search Result Types
Search Query Rules
Search Schema
Search Settings
Search Configuration Import
Search Configuration Export
Site collection features

c. Scroll down to 'SharePoint Server Publishing Infrastructure'.

d. Click on the 'Activate' button.

SharePoint Server Publishing Infrastructure
Provides centralized libraries, content types, master pages and page layouts and enables page scheduling and other publishing functionality for a site collection.   Activate

3. Go back to the home page Site Settings.

4. Select the new link 'Navigation' under 'Look and Feel'.

Look and Feel
Design Manager
Title, description, and logo
Device Channels
Navigation Elements
Change the look
Import Design Package
Navigation

5. Click on the 'Add Link' button in the Structural Navigation section.

Structural Navigation: Editing and Sorting
Use this section to reorder and modify the navigation items under this site. You can create, delete and edit navigation links and headings. You can also move navigation items under headings and choose to display or hide pages and subsites.

| | Move Up | Move Down | Edit | Delete | Add Heading... | Add Link... |

Look and Feel
Design Manager
Title, description, and logo
Device Channels
Navigation Elements
Change the look
Import Design Package
Navigation

Global Navigation
  Inventory
Current Navigation
  Home
  Notebook
  Documents
  Recent

6. Enter a title.

7. Enter the URL of the website you want the link to point to.

8. Select to open the link in a new window.

Navigation Link   ×

    Edit the title, URL, and description of the navigation item.

Title:	kalmstrom.com Business Solutions
URL:	http://www.kalmstrom.com Browse...
	☑ Open link in new window
Description:	
Audience:	

OK   Cancel

9. Click OK.

PHONE MESSAGES LIST

In this exercise we will create a custom list with the new experience interface. It will be used by a reception to handle messages about incoming phone calls, when the person who was called was not available.

We will start with creating a new list and add columns to it, and after that we will create suitable views for the list. The view that only shows unreturned calls will be added to the site homepage so that it can be seen easily.

Who called?		Phone number	Called	Returned
Susan ※	•••	49672991586	Jitu Patidar	No
Katarina ※	•••	10569034	Sumit Nandwal	No
Jane ※	•••	425938102	Kate Kalmström	No
Juan ※	•••	45937280	Kate Kalmström	No

Goal

Improve and automate the handling of phone messages. The reception previously managed those by writing post-its and handing them out manually. With SharePoint we can do better!

Actions

- Create a new list app that handles incoming phone messages. It should store:
  - Phone number
  - Name of caller
  - Called person – people or group
  - Call returned – yes/no
- Create Views
  - Today's phone calls
  - Not returned
  - Grouped per person called

Demo:

http://www.kalmstrom.com/Tips/SharePoint-Online-Exercises/Phone-Messages-Tracker.htm

➢ **Step 1, create a "Phone Messages" list app**

1. In a site where you want to add a Phone Messages list, click on the 'Site contents' link in the Quick Launch.

   Home

   Notebook

   Documents

   Pages

   Site contents

2. In the Site contents, click on '+ New' and select 'List'.

   ╋ New ⌄

   List

3. Enter the name "Phone Messages" in the pane that opens to the right.

4. Make sure that the box 'Show in site navigation' is checked.

   Create list

   Name

   | Phone Messages| ✕ |

   Description

   ☑ Show in site navigation

   Create   Cancel

5. Click on Create.

> **Step 2, change the Title into "Who called"**

1. In the Phone Messages list, click on the settings gear in the top navigation and select 'List settings'.

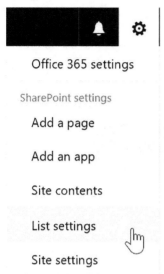

Office 365 settings

SharePoint settings

Add a page

Add an app

Site contents

List settings

Site settings

2. In the List settings page, click on the 'Title' link under 'Columns'.

Columns

A column stores information about each item in the list. The following columns are currently available in this list:

Column (click to edit)	Type	Required
Title	Single line of text	✓
Modified	Date and Time	
Created	Date and Time	
Created By	Person or Group	
Modified By	Person or Group	

3. Change the name 'Title' into 'Who called?'.

Settings ▸ Edit Column ⓘ

Name and Type

Type a name for this column.

Column name:

| Who called?| × |

The type of information in this column is:

Single line of text

4. Click OK.

5. Click on Phone Messages at the top of the settings page to go back to the list again.

> **Step 3, create a "Phone number" column**

1. Click on the plus sign in the Phone Messages list to to create a new list column.

2. Select 'Single line of text'.

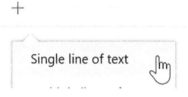

3. Enter the column name "Phone number".

New text column ✕

Name

Phone number   ✕

Create   Cancel

4. Click on 'Create'.

> **Step 4, create a "Called" column**

1. Click on the plus sign in the Phone Messages list.

2. Select 'Person'.

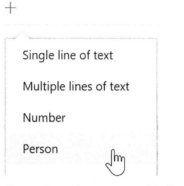

Single line of text

Multiple lines of text

Number

Person

3. Enter the column name "Called".

New person column   ×

Name

Called   ×

[Create]   Cancel

4. Click on 'Create'.

➢ **Step 5, create a "Returned" column**

1. Click on the plus sign in the Phone Messages list.

2. Select 'More…'.

\+

Single line of text

Multiple lines of text

Number

Person

Date

More…

3. A 'Create Column' page will open. Enter the column name "Returned".

Settings ▸ Create Column ⓘ

Name and Type	Column name:

Type a name for this column, and select the type of information you want to store in the column.

Column name:

Returned

The type of information in this column is:

○ Single line of text
○ Multiple lines of text
○ Choice (menu to choose from)
○ Number (1, 1.0, 100)
○ Currency ($, ¥, €)
○ Date and Time
○ Lookup (information already on this site)
◉ Yes/No (check box)
○ Person or Group
○ Hyperlink or Picture
○ Calculated (calculation based on other columns)
○ Task Outcome
○ External Data
○ Managed Metadata

Additional Column Settings

Specify detailed options for the type of information you selected.

Description:

Default value:

No ⌄

4. Check the radio button for the Yes/No column type.

5. Set the default value to No.

6. Click OK.

➢ **Step 6, fill out example data in the "Phone Messages" list**

1. Open the "Phone Messages" list in edit mode by clicking on the 'Quick edit' button in the command bar.

Phone Messages

✓ Who called? ∨		Phone number ∨	Called ∨	Returned ∨

2. Fill out fantasy names and telephone numbers for people who called.

3. Select names for people from your organization who might have been called.

4. Set at least one of the imaginary calls to returned by selecting Yes in the "Returned" column.

✓ Done

✓ Who called?	Phone number	Called	Returned	+
Susan 🗱	49672991586	Jitu Patidar	No	
Wolfgang 🗱	548216954	Peter Kalmström	Yes	
Katarina 🗱	10569034	Sumit Nandwal	No	
Jane 🗱	425938102	Kate Kalmström	No	
Juan 🗱	45937280	Kate Kalmström	No	
✎				

5. Click on 'Done' in the command bar to go back to the standard view.

Phone Messages

✓ Who called? ∨	Phone number ∨	Called ∨	Returned ∨
Susan	49672991586	Jitu Patidar	No
Wolfgang	548216954	Peter Kalmström	Yes
Katarina	10569034	Sumit Nandwal	No
Jane	425938102	Kate Kalmström	No
Juan	45937280	Kate Kalmström	No

➢ **Step 7, create a "Grouped by called" view**

1. Group the "Called" column by called.

Called ∨   Returned ∨

Jitu Pat...

    A to Z

Peter K

    Z to A

Sumit I

    Filter by   >

Kate K:

    Group by Called 🖑

    Column settings   >

2. Select 'Save view' in the command bar View selector.

+ New   📊 Export to Excel   ⌀ Flow ∨   ⬧ PowerApps ∨   · · ·   ☰ All Items* ∨   ⓘ

Phone Messages

                                                                                    ✓ All Items

∨ ∧   Who called? ∨   Phone number ∨   ⊞Called ∨   Returned ∨   +   Save view
                                                                                    Edit current view
     ∧ Called: Jitu Patidar (1)

          Susan   49672991586   Jitu Patidar   No

     ∧ Called: Kate Kalmström (2)

          Jane   425938102   Kate Kalmström   No

          Juan   45937280   Kate Kalmström   No

     ∧ Called: Peter Kalmström (1)

          Wolfgang   548216954   Peter Kalmström   Yes

     ∧ Called: Sumit Nandwal (1)

          Katarina   10569034   Sumit Nandwal   No

3. Give the new view a name.

                                              ×
    Save as

    Save current view or type a new name

    ┌─────────────────────────────────┐
    │ Grouped by Called   × │
    └─────────────────────────────────┘

    ✓ Make this a public view

            ┌──────────┐
            │   Save   │   Cancel
            └──────────┘

4. Click on 'Save'.

➢ Step 8, create a filtered "Not Returned" view

1. Go back to the "All items" view

2. Filter the "Returned" column by 'No', to show only the calls that have not been returned.

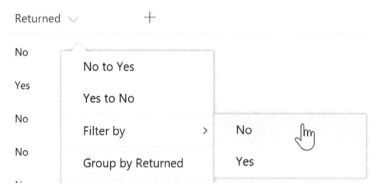

3. Select 'Save view' in the command bar View selector.

4. Give the new view a name, "Not Returned".

5. Click on 'Save'.

➢ Step 9, create a "Today's calls" view

1. Click on the settings gear in the top navigation and select 'List settings'.

2. At the bottom of the page, click on 'Create view'.

Views

A view of a list allows you

View (click to edit)

All Items

Grouped by Called

Not Returned

▫ Create view

3. Click on the Standard view type option.

Choose a view type

Standard View
View data on a Web page.

4. Give the new view a name.

Settings › Create View ⓘ

	OK	Cancel

Name

Type a name for this view of the list. Make the name descriptive, such as "Sorted by Author", so that site visitors will know what to expect when they click this link.

View Name:

Today's calls

☐ Make this the default view
(Applies to public views only)

5. Scroll down to 'Filter' and set the view to show items only when the column Created is equal to [Today].

⊟ Filter

Show all of the items in this view, or display a subset of the items by using filters. To filter on a column based on the current date or the current user of the site, type **[Today]** or **[Me]** as the column value. Use indexed columns in the first clause in order to speed up your view. Filters are particularly important for lists containing 5,000 or more items because they allow you to work with large lists more efficiently. Learn about filtering items.

○ Show all items in this view

◉ Show items only when the following is true:

Show the items when column

Created ∨

is equal to ∨

[Today]

6. Click OK

➢ **Step 10, add the "Not Returned" list view to the home page**

1. Go to the home page of the site where the Phone Messages app was created.

2. (Remove the default "Get started" content by clicking on 'REMOVE THIS'.)

Get started with your site   REMOVE THIS ⬅

3. Open the PAGE tab and click on the 'Edit' button.

4. Put the cursor where you want the app part to be placed.

5. Open the INSERT tab.

6. Click on the App Part button.

7. Select the Phone messages list.

8. Click on the Add button to the right on the page.

9. Edit the web part.

10. Select "Not Returned" in the Selected View dropdown.

◀ Phone Messages   ✕

List Views

You can edit the current view or select
another view.

Selected View

| Not Returned | ⌄ |

11. Click OK to the warning message.

12. (Hide the toolbar by selecting 'No Toolbar' under 'Toolbar Type'
    and expand the Appearance category and set the Chrome Type
    to 'None'.)

Toolbar Type

| No Toolbar | ⌄ |

Chrome Type

| None | ⌄ |

13. Click OK.

14. Save the page.

BROWSE   PAGE

Save   Check Out

Edit

SHAREPOINT CONTENT TYPES

Use content types to make sure that your SharePoint tenant contains the desired content and is managed in a consistent way. A content type is a reusable collection of metadata that describes the shared attributes and behaviors for a specific kind of content. Such content types can be defined for any item type, including documents, list items, media files, and folders.

In this exercise we will work with a content type for a site collection, and it will be used for documents in Project libraries in three subsites, Sales, Production and Support.

Before you start working on this exercise you need to have a site collection with three subsites: Sales, Production and Support. We created such a site collection in the first exercise, Create a SharePoint Intranet.

Goal

A project content type with metadata should be connected to libraries in three subsites. The same views and the same Word template should be used in all three libraries. Projects from the three sites should be displayed on the root page of the site collection.

Projects

Support	Sales	Production
Support Project 1	Sales Project 2	Production Project 1
	Sales Project 1	

Actions

- Create a content type that contains the following site columns:
  - Project manager – lookup against a new list of project managers
  - Start Date
  - End Date
  - Description
  - Status – choice
- Create a Sales Projects document library connected to the content type
- Create views in the Sales Projects library:
  - Overdue projects

- o   Grouped per project manager
- Create a Word template with Quick Parts information from the content type
- Save the Sales Projects library as a template.
- Use the template to create Projects libraries on the Production and Support sites.
- Show all projects on the root site in a Content Search or Content Query Web part.

Demo:

http://www.kalmstrom.com/Tips/SharePoint-Online-Exercises/Project-Content-Type.htm

> **Step 1, create a Project Managers list**

1. Open the Site Contents.

2. Click on '+ New' and select 'List'.

    $+$ New $\vee$

    List

3. In the 'Create List' pane, give the name "Project Managers" to the app.

    Create list

    Name

    | Project Managers | × |

    Description

    ☑ Show in site navigation

    Create   Cancel

4. Click on the Create button.

5. When the list has been created, click on Quick edit in the Quick Actions pane.

    🖉 Quick edit

6. Enter names of project managers.

✓ Done

✓ Title	+
Stina ✳	
Bertram ✳	
Adam ✳	

7. Click on Done in the Quick Actions pane.

➤ **Step 2, create a content type**

1. In the site collection **root page**, click on the settings icon at the top of the page and select 'Site settings'.

2. Under 'Web Designer Galleries' click on 'Site content types'.

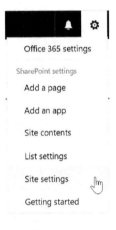

Office 365 settings

SharePoint settings

Add a page

Add an app

Site contents

List settings

Site settings

Getting started

Web Designer Galleries
Site columns
Site content types ←
Web parts
List templates

3. Click on the 'Create' link.

Site Settings ▸ Site Content Types

🖳 Create ◄━━━━

4. Fill out the form.

   a. Name: Project.

   b. Select 'Document Content Types' from the dropdown.

   c. Select 'Document' from the dropdown.

   d. Create a New group: Contoso.

New Site Content Type ⓘ

Name:

Project (a)

Description:

Parent Content Type:

Select parent content type from:

Document Content Types (b)

Parent Content Type:

Document (c)

Description:
Create a new document.

Put this site content type into:

○ Existing group:

Custom Content Types

● New group:

Contoso (d)   ×

5. Click OK.

➢ **Step 3, add columns to the content type**

1. Create a **Project Manager** column.

   a. At Site Content Types >Contoso, click on the link 'Add from **new** site column'.

Columns

Name

Name

Title

- Add from existing site columns
- Add from new site column ◄———
- Column order

b. Enter the name "Project Manager".

Column name:

Project Manager

The type of information in this column is:

○ Single line of text
○ Multiple lines of text
○ Choice (menu to choose from)
○ Number (1, 1.0, 100)
○ Currency ($, ¥, €)
○ Date and Time
◉ Lookup (information already on this site)

c. Select the radio button for 'Lookup (information already on this site)'.

d. Add the site column to the new group "Contoso".

Put this site column into:

○ Existing group:

Custom Columns ∨

◉ New group:

Contoso

e. Select to get information from the Project Managers list, Title column.

Get information from:

| Project Managers ∨ |

In this column:

| Title | ∨ |

    f.   Click OK.

2. Add Project Start and End Date columns.

    a.   At Site Content Types >Contoso, click on the link 'Add from **existing** site columns'.

Columns

Name

Title

Name

Description

Project Manager

▫ Add from existing site columns

    b.   Select the column Start Date and click on Add.

Select columns from:

| All Groups | ∨ |

Available columns:

| E-mail 2 |
| E-mail 3 |
| End Date |
| Enterprise Keywords |
| Errors |
| Event Address |
| Expenses |
| Export Job Size |

Add >

< Remove

Columns to add:

| Start Date |

    c.   Select the column End Date and click on Add.

    d.   Click OK.

3. Create a Project Description column.

    a.   At Site Content Types >Contoso, click on the link 'Add from **new** site column'.

    b.   Enter the name "Project Description".

c. Select the radio button for 'Multiple lines of text'.

d. Add the site column to the existing group "Contoso".

Put this site column into:

◉ Existing group:

Contoso ⌄

◯ New group:

e. Specify which type of text to allow.

Specify the type of text to allow:

◯ Plain text

◉ Enhanced rich text (Rich text with pictures, tables, and hyperlinks)

f. Click OK.

4. Create a **Status** column.

a. At Site Content Types >Contoso, click on the link "Add from **new** site column".

b. Enter the name "Project Status".

Column name:

Project Status

The type of information in this column is:

◯ Single line of text

◯ Multiple lines of text

◉ Choice (menu to choose from)

c. Select the radio button for 'Choice (menu to choose from)'.

d. Add the site column to the existing group "Contoso".

Type each choice on a separate line:

```
1. New
2. Ongoing
3. Delayed
4. Completed
```

Display choices using:

◉ Drop-Down Menu

◯ Radio Buttons

◯ Checkboxes (allow multiple selections)

Allow 'Fill-in' choices:

◯ Yes ◉ No

Default value:

◉ Choice ◯ Calculated Value

```
1. New
```

    e.   Click OK.

➢ **Step 4, create a Sales document library**

1. Go to the Sales subsite.

2. Click on Site contents.

3. Click on '+ New' and select 'App'.

+ New ⌄

List

Page

Document library

App

Subsite

4. Search for "Document".

5. Click on the Document library app.

Document Library

6. Enter the name "Sales Projects".

Adding Document Library   ×

Pick a name   Name:
You can add this app multiple times to your site. Give it a   Sales Projects   ×
unique name.

Advanced Options   Create   Cancel

7. Click on 'Create'.

8. In the Site Contents, click on the ellipsis at the new library and select "Settings".

📄 Sales Projects   · · ·   Document library

📄 Site Assets   Settings

9. Add the library app to the **Quick Launch** bar:

   a. Click on the link 'List name, description and navigation' under General Settings.

   General Settings

   ⊡ List name, description and navigation

   ⊡ Versioning settings

   b. Select Yes for 'Display this list on the Quick Launch?'.

c. Click on 'Save'.

➢ Step 5, connect the content type to the document library

1. In the Library Settings, click on 'Advanced settings' under General Settings.

General Settings

▫ List name, description and navigation

▫ Versioning settings

▫ Advanced settings ⟵

2. Select 'Yes' to allow management of content types.

Settings ▸ Advanced Settings

Content Types

Specify whether to allow the
management of content types on
this document library. Each
content type will appear on the
new button and can have a
unique set of columns, workflows
and other behaviors.

Allow management of content types?

● Yes   ○ No

3. Click OK.

4. In the new 'Content Types' group, click on 'Add from existing site content types'.

Content Types

This document library is configured to al

Content Type

Document

□ Add from existing site content types

5. Select the "Contoso" content types group.

Select site content types from:

Contoso ▾

Available Site Content Types: Content types to add:

Project

Add >

▸
Remove

6. Select the "Project" content type and click on Add.
7. Click OK.

➢ **Step 6, remove the default content type**

1. Click on 'Document' in the 'Content Types' section.

Content Types

This document library is configured to al

Content Type

Document

□ Add from existing site content types

2. Click on 'Delete this content type', so that only the "Project" content type is available for this library.

Settings

- Name and description
- Advanced settings
- Workflow settings
- Delete this content type
- Information management policy settings
- Document Information Panel settings

3. Click OK.

> **Step 7, add the content type columns to the default view**

1. At the bottom of the Library Settings page, click on 'All Documents' under 'Views'.

Views

A view of a document library ¡

View (click to edit)

All Documents

2. Check the boxes for the columns End Date, Start Date, Project Manager and Project Status and set the appropriate order.

☑	End Date	15 ∨
☐	File Size	16 ∨
☐	Folder Child Count	17 ∨
☐	ID	18 ∨
☐	ID of the User who has the Set the Protection Tag	19 ∨
☐	Item Child Count	20 ∨
☐	Name (for use in forms)	21 ∨
☐	Name (linked to document)	22 ∨
☐	Project Description	23 ∨
☑	Project Manager	24 ∨
☑	Project Status	25 ∨
☐	Protection Action	26 ∨
☐	Protection Tag	27 ∨
☐	Protection Tag Modified	28 ∨
☐	Record	29 ∨
☑	Start Date	14 ∨

3. Click OK.

➢ **Step 8, modify the Word template**

1. Open the Sales library and create a new item.

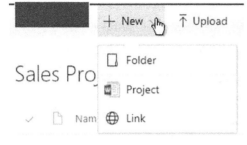

2. Edit the document in **Word**.

3. Insert a table with two columns. Make the right column wider.

4. Enter labels in the left column:

   a. Project Title

   b. Project Manager

   c. Start Date

   d. End Date

5. Enter the label "Description" under the table.

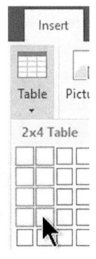

Project Title	
Project Manager	
Start Date	
End Date	

Description

6. Click in the first cell to the right, at "Project Title".

7. Click on the Quick Parts icon in the 'Text' ribbon group under the Insert tab.

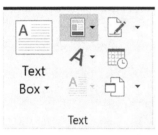

8. Select the Document Property 'Title' to add information from the content type in the first right column.

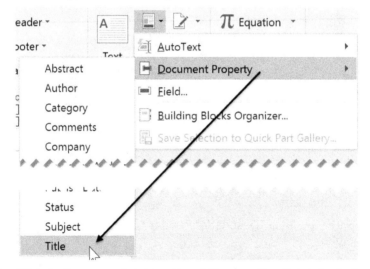

9. Click in the second right cell and then on the Quick Parts icon to select the Document Property 'Project Manager'.

10. Click in the third right cell and then on the Quick Parts icon to select the Document Property 'Start Date'.

11. Click in the fourth right cell and then on the Quick Parts icon to select the Document Property 'End Date'.

12. Click under the "Description" label and add the 'Project Description' property.

Project Title	[Title]
Project Manager	[Project Manager]
Start Date	2016-11-19
End Date	2016-11-19 12:40:00 PM

Description
⋮ Project Description

[Project Description]

13. Save the Word file to your desktop as "Project-Template.docx".

➢ Step 9, upload the template file to SharePoint

1. Go back to the home page of the Sales site.

2. Click on the settings gear and select "Site settings".

3. Click on 'Site content types' under Web Designer Galleries.

4. Select to show the group "Contoso".

Show Group: Contoso ▼

5.

6. Click on the "Project" content type.

7. Click on 'Advanced settings'.

8. Upload the file "Project-Template.docx".

⦿ Upload a new document template:

C:\Users\Peter\Desktop\Project Template.docx | Browse...

9.

10. Click OK.

➢ Step 10, test the template

1. To test the template, go to the Sales library.

2. Click on the 'Return to classic SharePoint' link below the Quick Launch.

Return to classic SharePoint

3. Create a new document.

Home   Sale
                    Create a new file   ✕
Produ
                    ▣ Project
⊕ New
All Documents   ▢ New folder
  ✓ ▢ Name

4. Edit the document in Word (to be able to use the content type fields).

5. Fill out the content type fields:

   a. Title: Sales Project 1

   b. Project Manager: select a name from the dropdown.

      If no names are displayed, open the File tab and click on the 'Show All Properties' link. Then show details for 'Project Manager' and select the project manager in the Details dialog instead.

Show All Properties   Project Manager   Show Details

Web File Properties   ?   ✕

Sales
Sales Projects
   Project Manager   [Adam   ⌄]
      Start Date   [11/19/2016]
                      Enter date in M/D/YYYY format.
        End Date   [11/19/2016]   [12 PM ⌄] [40 ⌄]
                      Enter date in M/D/YYYY format.
 Project Description [⌃
                              ○ ○
                                              ⌄]

    Project Status   [1. New   ⌄]

                                    [OK] [Cancel]

   This will give you a number instead of a name in the Word document, but the correct project manager name will show up in the Sales library column.

   c. Start Date

   d. End Date

e. Project Description

6. Save the project file.

> **Step 11, make additional library settings**

Open the LIBRARY tab and click on Library Settings and then 'Advanced settings' to make additional library settings:

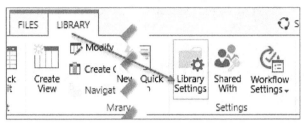

1. Always open items in the desktop version (of Word, in this case).

   Default open behavior for browser-enabled documents:

   ⦿ Open in the client application
   ○ Open in the browser
   ○ Use the server default (Open in the browser)

2. Use the classic experience interface for this library.

   Display this list using the new or classic experience?

   ○ Default experience set by my administrator
   ○ New experience
   ⦿ Classic experience

> **Step 12, create views**

1. A "Grouped by Project Manager" view:

   a. In the Sales library, click on 'Create View' under the views ellipsis.

   b. Select the Standard view.

53

Choose a view type

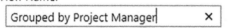
Standard View
View data on a Web page.

c. Enter the View Name "Grouped by Project Manager".

View Name:

Grouped by Project Manager   ✕

d. In the section Group By, select to group the items by Project Manager.

⊟ Group By

Select up to two columns to determine what type of group and subgroup the items in the view will be displayed in. Learn about grouping items.

First group by the column:

Project Manager

⦿ Show groups in ascending order (A, B, C, or 1, 2, 3)

◯ Show groups in descending order (C, B, A, or 3, 2, 1)

e. Click OK.

2. An "Overdue projects" view:

a. In the Sales library, click on 'Create View' under the views ellipsis.

b. Select the Standard view.

c. Enter the View Name "Overdue projects".

d. In the section Filter, set items to be shown only when the End Date is less than [Today] and the Status is not equal to 4. Completed.

⊟ Filter

Show all of the items in this view, or display a subset of the items by using filters. To filter on a column based on the current date or the current user of the site, type [Today] or [Me] as the column value. Use indexed columns in the first clause in order to speed up your view. Filters are particularly important for lists containing 5,000 or more items because they allow you to work with large lists more efficiently. Learn about filtering items.

◯ Show all items in this view

⦿ Show items only when the following is true:

Show the items when column

End Date

is less than

[Today]

⦿ And ◯ Or

When column

Project Status

is not equal to

4. Completed

e. Click OK.

➢ **Step 13, save the Sales Projects library as a template**

1. Click on "Library settings" under the LIBRARY tab.

2. Click on 'Save document library as template' in the Permissions and Management group.

Permissions and Management

▫ Delete this document library

▫ Save document library as template

3. Fill out the form.

    a. File name: Project Library.

    b. Template name: Project Library.

Settings › Save as Template ⓘ

File Name
Enter the name for this template file.

File name:

| Project Library |

Name and Description
The name and description of this template will be displayed on the Create page.

Template name:

| Project Library | × |

Template description:

| |

Include Content
Include content in your template if you want new document libraries created from this template to include the items in this

☐ Include Content

    c. Click OK.

4. Click OK to the message.

Sales › Operation Completed Successfully

The template has successfully been saved to the list template gallery. You can now create lists based on this template.

To manage templates in the gallery, go to the list template gallery.

To return to the list customization page, click **OK.**

| OK |

➢ **Step 14, create a Production Projects library from the template**

1. Go to the Production subsite.

2. Open the Site contents.

3. Click on '+ New and select App'.

4. Enter "project" in the search box.

| project | × |

3 apps match your search   Newest   Name

Issue Tracking
App Details

Access App
App Details

Project Library
App Details

5. Select the Project Library.

6. Enter the name "Production Projects".

7. Click on 'Create'.

8. Open the new library.

9. Under LIBRARY tab and click on Library Settings to make additional library settings that are not included in the template.

   a. Click on the link 'List name, description and navigation' under General Settings.

   b. Select Yes for "Display this list on the Quick Launch?".

   c. Click on Save.

   d. Click on 'Advanced settings'.

   e. Set the library to always open items in the desktop version (of Word, in this case).

   a. Set the library to use the classic experience.

   b. Click OK.

10. Click on '+ New' to create a new Project.

11. Check that the Project content type is shown and works.

➢ **Step 15, create a Support Projects library from the template**

1. Go to the Support subsite.

2. Open the Site contents.

3. Click on '+ New' and select 'App'.

4. Enter "project" in the search box.

5. Select the Project Library.

6. Enter the name "Support Projects".

7. Click on 'Create'.

8. Open the new library.

9. Under LIBRARY tab and click on Library Settings to make additional library settings that are not included in the template.

   a. Click on the link 'List name, description and navigation' under General Settings.

   b. Select Yes for 'Display this list on the Quick Launch?'.

   c. Click on 'Save'.

   d. Click on 'Advanced settings'.

   e. Set the library to always open items in the desktop version (of Word, in this case).

   f. Set the library to use the classic experience.

   g. Click OK.

10. Click on '+ New' to create a new Project.

11. Check that the Project content type is shown and works.

> **Step 16, show all projects in a Content Search web part on the root site**

(only for Office 365 E3 and E5 subscriptions)

Home   Sales   Production   Support

kDemo Intranet

Home
Notebook
Documents
Recent
Phone Messages
Customers
Countries
Project Managers

Projects

📄 Sales Project 2

📄 Production Project 1

📄 Support Project 1

📄 Sales Project 1

1. Go to the **root site** of the site collection.

2. Click on the 'EDIT' icon on top right.

 ☆ FOLLOW ✏ EDIT 🔲

3. Place the mouse cursor where you want to add the web part.

4. Click on 'Web Part' under the INSERT tab.

5. Select 'Content Rollup'.

6. Select 'Content Search'.

7. Click on Add.

8. Click on 'Edit Web Part'.

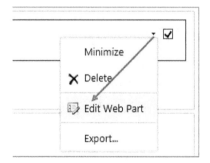

9. Expand the Appearance section:

   a. Change the title to "Projects".

   b. Change the Crome Type to 'Title and Border'.

Chrome Type

Title and Border ∨

10. Change the other properties:

    a. Show 50 items

    b. Select the 'List with Paging' control

◀ Content Search   ✕

Properties   ☆

    ⊟ Search Criteria   Help

    Change query   (d)

    Number of items to show

    50   (a)

    ⊟ Display Templates   Help

    Control

    List with Paging (b)   ∨

    Item

    Two lines (c)   ∨

    c. Show items in 'Two lines'.

    d. Click on the 'Change query' button.

11. Build a query that filters what content should be displayed in the web part:

    a. Search by 'Items matching a content type (System)'.

    b. Restrict the search to the 'Current site collection'.

    c. Restrict the search to the content type 'Project'.

Build Your Query

BASICS   REFINERS   SETTINGS   TEST

Switch to Advanced Mode

Select a query
Choose what content you want to search by
selecting a result source.

Items matching a content type (System) ☑ (a)

Restrict by app
You can scope the search results to a specific
site, library, list or URL.

Current site collection ☑ (b)

Restrict by tag
You can limit results to content tagged with
specific terms, including site navigation terms.

● Don't restrict by any tag
○ Restrict by navigation term of current
page
○ Restrict by current and child navigation
terms
○ Restrict on this tag: [   ]

Restrict by content type
You can limit results to a particular content
type and all those that inherit from it.

Project ☑ (c)

d. Click OK to the Query Builder.

12. Click Apply to the web part properties.

⊞ Advanced		
OK	Cancel	Apply

13. Save the page.

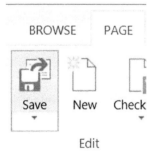

BROWSE   PAGE

Save   New   Check

Edit

60

(only for Office 365 E3 and E5 subscriptions)

Projects

Support	Sales	Production
Support Project 1	Sales Project 2	Production Project 1
	Sales Project 1	

1. Go to the **root site** of the site collection.

2. Click on the settings gear at the top of the page and select 'Site settings'.

3. Under 'Site Collection Administration', click on the link "Site collection features".

Site Collection Administration
Recycle bin
Search Result Sources
Search Result Types
Search Query Rules
Search Schema
Search Settings
Search Configuration Import
Search Configuration Export
Site collection features

4. Activate SharePoint Server Publishing Infrastructure

SharePoint Server Publishing Infrastructure
Provides centralized libraries, content types, master pages and page layouts and enables page scheduling and other publishing functionality for a site collection.

Activate

5. On the root site, click on the 'EDIT' icon on top right.

☆ FOLLOW ✏ EDIT ⧉

6. Place the mouse cursor where you want to add the web part to be placed.

7. Click on 'Web Part' under the 'INSERT' tab.

8. Select 'Content Rollup'.

9. Select 'Content Query'.

10. Click on 'Add'.

11. Click on "Edit Web Part".

12. Expand 'Query'.

   a. Under 'List Type', select 'Document Library'.

   b. Under 'Content Type', select "Contoso Content Types" and then "Project".

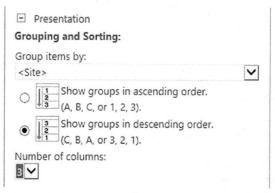

13. Expand 'Presentation'.

    a.   Group items by <Site>.

    b.   Number of columns: 3.

14. Expand 'Appearance' and change the title to "Projects".

15. Click on 'Apply'.

16. Click on 'SAVE' in the top right corner of the page.

Document Library Templates

Use templates for Office documents in SharePoint libraries! That way a company logo and other required information or design features will be included in each document that is created from the library.

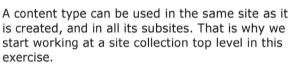

In this exercise we will create three site content types and add an Office template to each of them: Excel, PowerPoint and Word. Then we will add these content types to a library and remove the default content type. When we are satisfied with the library, we will save it as a library template.

Now the new template will show up among the other templates when you create a new app, so that we can use it to create other libraries through the whole site collection.

Contoso Document library
App Details

A content type can be used in the same site as it is created, and in all its subsites. That is why we start working at a site collection top level in this exercise.

Note: the exercise will *not* work on the default site collection of SharePoint Online, because that site does not have scripting enabled. Team sites in other site collections have scripting enabled by default, and you may of course activate scripting on the default site collection too. *Refer to* http://www.kalmstrom.com/Tips/SharePoint-Online-Course/Allow-Custom-Script-In-SharePoint.htm.

I advice you to use Internet Explorer for this exercise. Opening Office applications does not always work well with other web browsers. When this is written, you must also use the desktop Office and the classic library experience interface.

This exercise shows the classic experience interface, but the features work in the new experience too.

Before you start this exercise, you need to prepare:

- Three Office files, Excel, PowerPoint and Word, that you can use as templates. It does not have to be actual template files. Any .xlsx, .pptx and .docx files will do.
- An empty SharePoint document library.

Goal

When you create new documents from a SharePoint library, a blank template is used by default. We need to change that, so that all new documents use the company theme and templates.

Steps

- Create three new content types in their own content type group: Contoso Doc, Contoso Presentation and Contoso Spreadsheet
- Add all three content types to a document library
- Set "Contoso Doc" as the new default content type and remove the default "Document" content type
- Save the document library app as a template under the name "Contoso Doc Lib"

Demo:

http://www.kalmstrom.com/Tips/SharePoint-Online-Exercises/Create-Library-Template.htm

➢ **Step 1, create new site content types with Office templates**

1. "Contoso **Doc**"

   a. In the site collection **root page**, click on the settings icon at the top of the page and select 'Site settings'.

   b. Under the "Web Designer Galleries" click on "Site content types".

   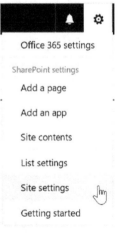

   Web Designer Galleries
   Site columns
   Site content types ⬅
   Web parts
   List templates

   c.

   d. Click on the 'Create' link and fill out the form.

   # Site Settings ▸ Site Content Types

   🖼 Create ⬅━━━━━

e. Enter the name "Contoso Doc".

Site Content Types · New Site Content Type ⓘ

Name and Description

Type a name and description for this content type. The description will be shown on the new button.

Name:

    Contoso Doc

Description:

Parent Content Type:

Select parent content type from:

    Document Content Types   ▾

Parent Content Type:

    Document   ▾

Description:
Create a new document.

Group

Specify a site content type group. Categorizing content types into groups will make it easier for users to find them.

Put this site content type into:

○ Existing group:

    Custom Content Types   ▾

◉ New group:

    Contoso Content Types

OK   Cancel

f. Select 'Document Content Types' from the dropdown.

g. Select 'Document' from the dropdown.

h. Select the 'New group' option.

i. Enter the group name "Contoso Content Types".

j. Click OK.

k. Click on 'Advanced settings'.

Settings

▫ Name, description, and group

▫ Advanced settings ◀━━━

▫ Workflow settings

▫ Delete this site content type

l. Select the 'Upload a new document template' option.

m. Click on 'Browse…'.

n. Select your Word template.

Site Content Type · Advanced Settings ⓘ

Document Template

Specify the document template for this content type.

○ Enter the URL of an existing document template:

⦿ Upload a new document template:

| C:\Users\rituka\Desktop\ContosoDoc.docx | Browse... |

Read Only

Choose whether the content type is modifiable. This setting can be changed later from this page by anyone with permissions to edit this type.

Should this content type be read only?

○ Yes

⦿ No

Update Sites and Lists

Specify whether all child site and list content types using this type should be updated with the settings on this page. This operation can take a long time, and any customizations made to the child site and list content types will be lost.

Update all content types inheriting from this type?

⦿ Yes

○ No

OK   Cancel

o. Click on 'Open'.

p. Click OK

2. "Contoso **Spreadsheet**"

a. Go to the root site of the SharePoint site collection.

b. Click on the settings icon at the top of the page and select 'Site settings'.

c. Click on 'Site content types' under 'Web Designer Galleries'.

d. Click on 'Create'.

e. Enter the name "Contoso Spreadsheet".

f. Select 'Document Content Types' from the dropdown.

g. Select 'Document' from the dropdown.

h. Select the 'Existing group' option.

i. Select "Contoso Content Types" from the dropdown.

j. Click OK.

k. Click on 'Advanced settings'.

l. Select the 'Upload a new document template' option.

m. Click on 'Browse...'.

n. Select your Excel template.

o. Click on Open.

p. Click OK

3. "Contoso Presentation"

a. Go to the root site of the SharePoint site collection.

b. Click on the settings icon at the top of the page and select 'Site settings'.

c. Click on 'Site content types' under 'Web Designer Galleries'.

d. Click on 'Site Content Types'.

e. Click on 'Create'.

f. Enter the name "Contoso Presentation".

g. Select 'Document Content Types' from the dropdown.

h. Select 'Document' from the dropdown.

i. Select the 'Existing group' option.

j. Select "Contoso Content Types "from the dropdown.

k. Click OK.

l. Click on 'Advanced settings'.

m. Select the 'Upload a new document template' option.

n. Click on 'Browse...'.

o. Select your PowerPoint template.

p. Click on 'Open'.

q. Click OK

> **Step 2, add the content types to the document library**

1. Open the 'LIBRARY' tab and click on 'Library Settings'.

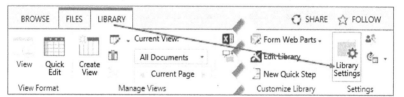

2. Click on 'Advanced settings'.

General Settings

- List name, description and navigation
- Versioning settings
- Advanced settings ←

3. Select 'Yes' to allow management of content types.

Settings ▸ Advanced Settings

Content Types

Specify whether to allow the management of content types on this document library. Each content type will appear on the new button and can have a unique set of columns, workflows and other behaviors.

Allow management of content types?

◉ Yes   ◯ No

4. Set documents to open in the client application.

   Default open behavior for browser-enabled documents:

   ◉ Open in the client application
   ◯ Open in the browser
   ◯ Use the server default (Open in the browser)

5. Click OK.

6. In the new 'Content Types' group in the settings page, click on 'Add from existing site content types'.

   Content Types

   This document library is configured to al

   Content Type

   Document

   ▫ Add from existing site content types

7. Select "Contoso Content Types" from the dropdown.

8. Select all the three Content Types you have created:

   a. Contoso Doc

   b. Contoso Presentation

   c. Contoso Spreadsheet

Settings · Add Content Types ⓘ

Select Content Types

Select from the list of available site content types to add them to this list.

Select site content types from:

Contoso Content Types ▾

Available Site Content Types:

Contoso Doc
Contoso Presentation
Contoso Spreadsheet

Add >

< Remove

Content types to add:

Description:
None

Group: Contoso Content Types

OK   Cancel

9. Click on the 'Add' button.

10. Click OK.

> **Step 3, remove the default "Document" content type**

1. Click on the default content type 'Document' in the 'Content Types' section.

Content Types

This document library is configured to al

Content Type

Document ⬅

▫ Add from existing site content types

2. Click on 'Delete this content type', so that only the "Contoso Doc, Contoso Presentation, and Contoso Spreadsheet" content types are available for this library.

Settings

- Name and description
- Advanced settings
- Workflow settings
- Delete this content type
- Information management policy settings
- Document Information Panel settings

3. Click OK.

> **Step 4, save the document library app as a template**

1. In the library, open the 'LIBRARY' tab and click on 'Library settings'.
2. Click on 'Save document library as template'.

Permissions and Management

- Delete this document library
- Save document library as template

3. Enter the file name "Contoso Document library".
4. Enter the template name "Contoso Document library".
5. Click OK.

SharePoint Resource Booking System

SharePoint calendar apps can be used for simple resource booking. In such a solution each resource has its own calendar, and users book a resource by creating an event for the suitable date and time in the resource's calendar.

When you connect the resource calendars to a list app and add a column for that app in the calendar form, it will also be possible to book extras with each reservation.

In this exercise we will create such resource calendar apps connected to a services list. We will add all calendars to an overlay view by opening one of the calendars and adding the other calendars to the save view. The first calendar can then be renamed to "Resouce booking", and that way users only have one link to click on to see all calendars.

When users connect resource calendars to Outlook, they can book from Outlook without visiting the SharePoint site.

Goal

Create a resource booking system, to handle room reservations and bookings of services. Show all calendars in one list view. Connect one calendar to Outlook.

Actions

- Create a new custom list app with the services offered:

- o Coffee
- o High Tea
- o Lunch
- o Dinner and entertainment
- Create a calendar list app for the "Sweden" room. It should have a column for multi-value lookup against the Services list app
- Save the "Sweden" calendar list as a template
- Create calendar list apps based on this template for the other meeting rooms: Estonia, India, Spain and USA
- Add all the calendars to one overlay view and link only that view from the QuickLaunch
- Connect the "India" calendar to Outlook

Demo:

http://www.kalmstrom.com//Tips/SharePoint-Online-Exercises/SharePoint-Online-Resource-Booking.htm

> **Step 1, create a Services list app**

1. Open the Site Contents.
2. Click on "New" and select "List".

+ New ∨

List

Page

3. Enter the Name "Services".
4. Make sure the box for "Show in site navigation" is checked.

Create list

Name

Services   ×

Description

☑ Show in site navigation

Create   Cancel

5. Click on "Create".

6. When the list has been created, click on Quick edit in the Quick Actions pane.

   ✎ Quick edit

7. Enter in the Services:

   a. Coffee

   b. High Tea

   c. Lunch

   d. Dinner and Entertainment

✓	Title	+
	Coffee ✻	
	High Tea ✻	
	Lunch ✻	
	Dinner and entertainment ✻	

8. Click on Done in the Quick Actions pane.

➤ **Step 2, create a "Sweden" calendar app**

1. Open the Site Contents.

2. Click on New and select App.

   + New ⌄

   List

   Page

   Document library

   App

   Subsite

3. Search for 'Calendar'.

4. Select the Calendar app.

Calendar

5. Give the name "Sweden" to the app.

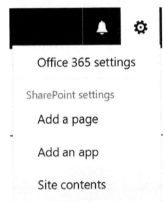

6. Click on the Create button.

> **Step 3, add the "Sweden" calendar to the Quick Launch**

1. Click on the settings gear and open the Site contents.

Office 365 settings

SharePoint settings

Add a page

Add an app

Site contents

2. Find the new "Sweden" calendar and click on it to open.

Sweden   Events list

3. Click on 'List Settings' under the 'CALENDAR' tab.

4. Under General Settings, click on 'List name, description and navigation'.

General Settings

▫ List name, description and navigation

5. Select the radio button Yes to display the list on the Quick Launch.

6. Click on 'Save'.

Navigation

Specify whether a link to this list appears in the Quick Launch. Note: it only appears if Quick Launch is used for navigation on your site.

Display this list on the Quick Launch?

◉ Yes ○ No

[Save] [Cancel]

> **Step 4, create a "Services Booked" column in the "Sweden" calendar**

1. Click on the "Sweden" calendar in the Quick Launch.

2. Open the 'CALENDAR' tab.

3. Click on "Create Column".

4. Enter the Column Name "Services Booked".

5. Select "Lookup (information already on this site)".

6. Select to get information from the "Services" list.

7. Select the "Title" column.

8. Check "Allow multiple values".

9. Click OK.

10. Check the column:

    a. Go to the "Events" tab'

    b. Click on 'New Event'.

c. Make sure you can add services.

Recurrence	☐ Make this a rep...ent.		
Services Booked	Dinner and Entertainmer High Tea	Add >	Coffee Lunch
		< Remove	
			Save Cancel

> **Step 5, save the "Sweden" calendar as a template**

1. Open the ribbon "Calendar" tab.
2. Click on "List Settings".
3. Click on "Save list as template".

Permissions and Management

- Delete this list

- Save list as template

4. Fill out the fields.
   a. File name: ResourceCalendar
   b. Template name: ResourceCalendar

Settings · Save as Template ⓘ

File Name
Enter the name for this template file.

File name:
ResourceCalendar

Name and Description
The name and description of this template
will be displayed on the Create page.

Template name:
ResourceCalendar

Template description:

5. Click OK.
6. Click on OK to the message.

Operation Completed Successfully

The template has successfully been saved to the list template gallery. You can now create lists based on this template.

To manage templates in the gallery, go to the list template gallery.

To return to the list customization page, click **OK**.

OK

> ## Step 6, create a "USA" resource calendar

1. Open the Site Contents.
2. Click on '+ New' and select 'App'.
3. Search for "Resource".
4. Click on "ResourceCalendar".
5. Enter the name "USA".
6. Click on 'Create'.

> ## Step 7, create a "Spain" resource calendar

1. Open the Site Contents.
2. Click on '+ New' and select 'App'
3. Search for "Resource".
4. Click on "ResourceCalendar".
5. Enter the name "Spain".
6. Click on 'Create'.

> ## Step 8, create an "India" resource calendar

1. Open the Site Contents.
2. Click on '+ New' and select 'App'.
3. Search for "Resource".
4. Click on "ResourceCalendar".
5. Enter the name "India".
6. Click on 'Create'.

> ## Step 9, create an "Estonia" resource calendar

1. Open the Site Contents.
2. Click on '+ New' and select 'App'.

3. Search for "Resource".

4. Click on "ResourceCalendar".

5. Enter the name "Estonia".

6. Click on 'Create'.

➢ Step 10, add all calendars to an Overlay view

1. Open the calendar "Sweden".

2. Click on 'Calendars Overlay' under the CALENDAR tab.

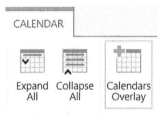

3. Add the calendar "India" to the Calendars Overlay.

   a. Click on 'New Calendar'.

   b. Fill out the Calendar Name: India.

   c. Select color.

   d. Click on 'Resolve'.

   e. Select "'India' from the List dropdown.

   f. Select 'Calendar' from the List View dropdown.

   g. Check 'Always show'.

   h. Click OK.

Calendar Name:

India

The type of calendar is:

⦿ SharePoint

◯ Exchange

Description:

Color:

Dark Teal, #00485b ⌄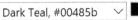

Web URL:

https://kalmstromnet.sharepoint.com/sites/Kate   Resolve

List:

India ⌄

List View:

Calendar ⌄

☑ Always show

4. Add the calendar "Estonia" to the Calendars Overlay.

   a. Click on 'New Calendar'.

   b. Fill out the Calendar Name: Estonia

   c. Select color.

   d. Click on 'Resolve'.

   e. Select 'Estonia' from the List dropdown.

   f. Select 'Calendar' the List View dropdown.

   g. Check 'Always show'.

   h. Click OK.

5. Add the calendar "USA" to the Calendars Overlay.

   a. Click on 'New Calendar'

   b. Fill out the Calendar Name: USA.

   c. Select Color.

d. Click on 'Resolve'.

e. Select 'USA' from the List dropdown.

f. Select 'Calendar' from the List View dropdown.

g. Check 'Always show'.

h. Click OK.

6. Add the calendar "Spain" to the Calendars Overlay.

    a. Click on 'New Calendar'.

    b. Fill out the Calendar Name: Spain.

    c. Select Color.

    d. Click on 'Resolve'.

    e. Select 'Spain' from the List dropdown.

    f. Select 'Calendar' from the List View dropdown.

    g. Check 'Always show'.

    h. Click OK.

    i. Again click OK.

7. Check if the booking works by clicking a date in one of the calendars, make a booking and see that it shows up in the correct calendar.

➢ **Step 11, rename the "Sweden" calendar**

1. Go to the site home page.

2. Click on 'EDIT LINKS' at the bottom of the Quick Launch.

    ✎ EDIT LINKS

3. Click on the "Sweden" link and rename it to "Room booking".

➢ **Step 12, connect one of the resource calendars to Outlook**

1. Open the "India" calendar.

2. Under the ribbon 'CALENDAR' tab, click on 'Connect to Outlook.

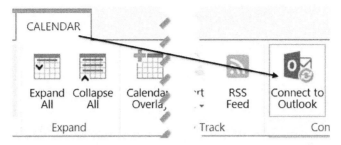

3. Click Yes to both warning messages.

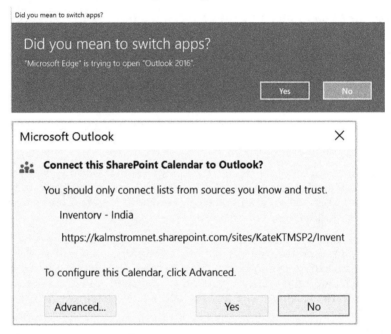

4. Enter your password.

5. Check 'Remember my credentials'.

6. Click OK.

7. Check the connection by creating an event.

CONNECT APP PARTS

Web parts and app parts are used in all kinds of site pages. The two terms are often confused even inside SharePoint, but they are used in the same way: to make it possible to add different kinds of content to a page.

When you create a list or library in a SharePoint site, it will automatically also be available as an app part that can be inserted in a wiki or web part page. Two such app parts can be connected on the same page.

Wiki pages and web part pages are created through the Site Pages library under Site Contents.

Before you start working with this exercise you need to have an Excel file with two tables, one with some customer data and one with countries. Design the default view as you prefer, but it must be a standard view for both lists, not a datasheet view.

If you want to use my Excel file, you are welcome to download it: http://www.kalmstrom.com/Tips/SharePoint-Online-Exercises/files/Customers.xlsx

Note that data can only be updated in SharePoint when you export from Excel to SharePoint with the Excel Export button, as we do in this exercise. Changes in SharePoint can be transferred to Excel by using the Excel Refresh button, but not vice versa.

The task is to export two Excel tables, Countries and Customers, to SharePoint. That creates two lists with the same names. The lists have the classic experience interface, and the default view is a datasheet. We have to change the view into standard, and then we will create a wiki page with two columns and add the app parts Customer and Country to it.

Finally we will connect the two app parts on the page, so that the Customers list is filtered by the selected country. When that is done, you can click on the icon to the left of a country and see only the customers from that country to the right.

Countries

☐	Type	Country
▣	▯	Argentina ☐ NEW
▣	▯	Austria ☐ NEW
▣	▯	Belgium ☐ NEW
▣	▯	Brazil ☐ NEW
▣	▯	Canada ☐ NEW
▣	▯	Denmark ☐ NEW
▣	▯	Finland ☐ NEW

Customers

☐	Type	CustomerID	CustomerName	Contact first name	Contact last name
	▯	MAISD ☐ NEW	Maison Dewey	Catherine	Dewey
	▯	SUPRD ☐ NEW	Suprêmes délices	Pascale	Cartrain

If you get problems performing the last step of this exercise, the actual connection of the two app parts, I recommend that you copy the link to the page with the two columns and paste it in another browser. Which browser works depends on your pop-up-blocking settings and several other factors. As soon as you have made the connection, it will work in your favorite browser also.

Goal

Import Excel tables to SharePoint lists and create a site page where the app parts of the two new lists are connected.

Actions

- Create two new SharePoint lists by importing one Excel table with customer details and one with just the countries from the customer details table
- Make the standard view default for both lists
- Create a new wiki page with two columns
- Add two list app parts to the page
- Connect the two app parts, so that when a country is clicked, only customers from that country are visible

Demo:

http://www.kalmstrom.com/Tips/SharePoint-Online-Exercises/Connect-App-Parts.htm

➢ **Step 1, format the "Customers" list as a table**

1. In Excel, if the range of customer data is not already formatted as a table, remove all blank rows and columns inside the data range.

2. Click in the range of data and then on the 'Format as Table' button under the 'Home' tab.

3. Click OK.

Format As Table   ? ✕

Where is the data for your table?

=$A$1:$M$92

☑ My table has headers

OK   Cancel

➢ **Step 2, export the "Customers" table to SharePoint**

1. Click on the 'Export' table button under the new 'Design' tab and select 'Export Table to SharePoint List...'

| as | Data | Review | View | Design |

Export Refresh

Properties

Open in Browser

Unlink

☑ Hea

☐ Tota

☑ Ban

Export Table to SharePoint List...

2. Go to the **SharePoint** site where you want to create the two lists and copy its URL.

3. In **Excel**, paste the SharePoint site URL in the Export step 1 dialog.

4. Check the box for 'Create a read-only connection to the new SharePoint list'.

5. Enter a name (and a description).

6. Click on 'Next' to reach step 2.

7. Click on 'Finish'. (Nothing can be changed in the step 2 dialog.

Export Table to SharePoint List - Step 2 of 2   ?   X

To publish to a SharePoint list, Excel must force columns to use certain recognized data types. All cells with individual formulas will be converted to values.

Verify that each of the columns listed below is associated with the correct data type. If a column is associated with an incorrect data type, click Cancel and confirm that the key cell can be converted to the correct type.

Column	Data Type	Key Cell
CustomerID	Text (single line)	
CustomerName	Text (single line)	
Contact first name	Text (single line)	
Contact last name	Text (single line)	
E-mail	Text (single line) [Formulas removed]	
Gender	Text (single line)	
Contact Title	Text (single line)	
Address	Text (single line)	

Help	Cancel	Back	Next	Finish

8. Click OK to the success message.

Microsoft SharePoint Foundation   ?   X

The table was successfully published and may be viewed on:

https://kalmstromnet.sharepoint.com/sites/KateKTMSP2/Li...

OK

> **Step 3, export the "Countries" table to SharePoint**

1. In Excel, if the range of customer data is not formatted as a table, click in the range of data and then on the 'Format as Table' button under the 'Home' tab.

2. Click OK.

3. Click on the 'Export' button under the new 'Design' tab and select 'Export Table to SharePoint List…'

4. Go to the SharePoint site where you want to create the two lists and copy its URL.

5. Paste the URL in the Export step 1 dialog.

6. Enter a name (and a description).

7. Click on 'Next' to reach step 2.

88

8. Click on 'Finish'.

9. Click on the link in the success message to reach the new "Countries" list.

> **Step 4, create a default standard view in the "Countries" list**

1. In the **SharePoint** "Countries" list, click on 'Create View' under the view ellipsis.

Countries

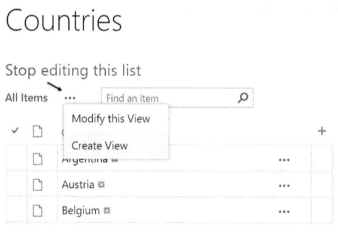

2. Select the Standard view.

   Choose a view type

   Standard View
   View data on a Web page.

3. Enter the View Name "Countries".

4. Check the box for 'Make this the default view'.

Settings ▸ Create View ⓘ

OK	Cancel

Name

Type a name for this view of the list. Make the name descriptive, such as "Sorted by Author", so that site visitors will know what to expect when they click this link.

View Name:

Countries

☑ Make this the default view
(Applies to public views only)

5. Click OK.

➢ Step 5, create a default standard view in the "Customers" list

1. Click on the settings gear and select 'Site Ccontents'.

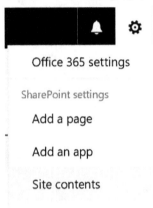

2. Under 'Contents', find the "Customers" list you just created from an Excel table.

3. Open the "Customers" list.

4. Click on 'Create View' under the view ellipsis.

5. Select the Standard view.

6. Enter the View Name "Customers".

7. Check the box for 'Make this the default view'.

8. Click OK.

➢ Step 6, create a new wiki page with two columns

1. Click on the settings icon at the top of any page and select 'Site contents'.

2. In the Site Contents, open the Site Pages library.

3. Click on '+New' in the command bar.

4. Select 'Wiki Page'.

5. Enter the New page name "Customers-Countries".

New Item

New page name:

| Customers-Countries | × |

Find it at https://kalmstromnet.sharepoint.com/sites/KateKTMSP2/SitePages/Customers-Countries.aspx

Create   Cancel

6. Click on 'Create'.

7. The new page will open in edit mode.

8. Click on the 'Text Layout' button under the 'FORMAT TEXT' tab in the ribbon and select 'Two columns'.

➤ **Step 7, add an App Part to display information from the "Countries" list**

1. In the wiki page edit mode, click in the left column.

2. Open the ribbon 'INSERT' tab.

3. Click on the 'App Part' button.

4. Select "Countries".

5. Click on the 'Add' button.

> **Step 8, add an App part to display information from the "Customers" list**

1. In the wiki page edit mode, click in the right column.

2. Open the ribbon 'INSERT' tab.

3. Click on the 'App Part' button.

4. Click on "Customers".

5. Click on the 'Add' button.

6. Save the page (in case you get trouble with the next step).

> **Step 9, connect the two app parts**

1. Click on the 'EDIT' link at the top right to open the page in edit mode again.

2. Expand the tool pin accordion in the top right corner of the "Countries" app part and click on 'Edit Web Part'.

3. Again expand the tool pin accordion and click on 'Edit Web Part'.

4. Select 'Connections' > 'Send Row of Data To' > 'Customers'.

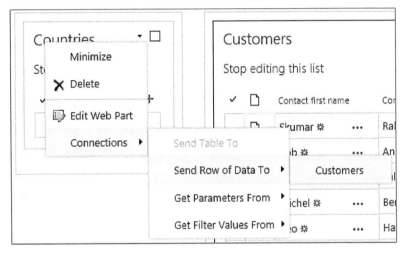

5. Under the Choose Connection tab, select 'Get Filter Values From'.

6. Click on 'Configure'.

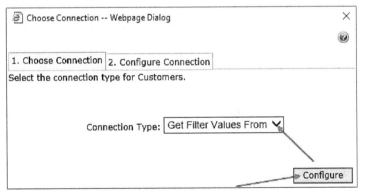

7. Select "Country" from the dropdowns.

Configure Connection -- Webpage Dialog   ✕

| 1. Choose Connection | 2. Configure Connection |

Connection Settings

Provider Field Name: | Country   ∨ |
Consumer Field Name: | Country   ∨ |

[Finish]   [Cancel]

8. Click on 'Finish'.

9. Click on 'SAVE' in the top right corner of the page.

☆ FOLLOW   🖫 SAVE   ⬚

WORKFLOW THAT SENDS E-MAIL NOTIFICATIONS ABOUT HIGH PRIORITY TASKS

When you work with tasks in SharePoint it is convenient to get an e-mail notification if someone has created a task with high priority for you. When that e-mail also contains a link to the task you can open the task quickly.

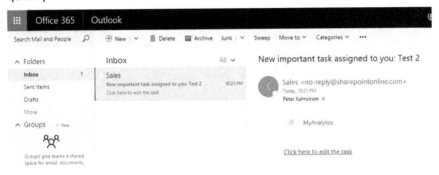

Such e-mail notifications can be sent automatically if you create a SharePoint workflow for the Tasks list, and that is what we will do in this exercise. Workflows are limited to sites and stored there, and they are created in SharePoint Designer.

Before you start working with the exercise, you need to make sure you have SharePoint Designer installed. To install SharePoint Designer 2013 from within Office 365, click on the Settings gear on any page in Office 365 and open the Office 365 settings.

1. Open the Software section.

2. Open Tools & add-ins to find SharePoint Designer 2013.

3. Click on Download and Install. You are now re-directed to a Download center that opens in a new window.

4. Download and Run the file.

Goal

Create a workflow that sends an e-mail notifying the assignee of a high priority task

Actions

- Open a SP 2013 Team site in SharePoint Designer 2013
- Create a new Tasks app list
- Create a new 2013 list workflow that runs on tasks created
- If a task priority is High, send an e-mail to "Assigned To" about it

- Add the task name in the e-mail subject
- Insert a hyperlink to the Edit Item form in the e-mail body: https://site.com/lists/Tasks/EditForm.aspx?ID=1

Demo:

http://www.kalmstrom.com/Tips/SharePoint-Online-Exercises/Notifications-Workflow.htm

> **Step 1, open the site in SharePoint Designer 2013**

1. In the **SharePoint** site where you want to add the workflow, right click on the SharePoint icon and copy the URL to the site.

Team Site

Open in new tab

Home

News

Open in new window

Save target as

Product document

Notebook

Copy link

2. Open SharePoint Designer 2013.

3. Click on the 'Open Site' button.

4. Paste the link you copied in the Site name field.

5. Click on 'Open'.

Open Site

6. Log in to the site.

7. Click on 'Open' again.

> **Step 2, create a Tasks list**

1. In SharePoint Designer 2013, click on the 'SharePoint List' button and select the Tasks list.

SITE

| SharePoint List ▾ | Document Library ▾ | List Workflow ▾ | Reusa Workf |

Generic Lists

Announcements

Calendar

Contacts

Custom List

Custom List in Datasheet View

Discussion Board

Promoted Links

Links

Tasks

2. Give the new list a name.

Create list or document library   ?   ×

Add a new list or document library to your site

Enter a name and description

Name:

Tasks

Description:

OK   Cancel

3. Click OK.

4. Make the preferred list settings.

Settings

General settings for this list.

General Settings

☑ Display this list on the Quick Launch

☐ Hide from browser

Advanced Settings

☑ Allow attachments

☐ Require content approval for submitted items

☑ Create a version each time you edit an item

☑ Allow management of content types

➢ **Step 3, create a new workflow for the Task list**

1. At Workflows, click on the New button.

Workflows   ⏲ **New...**   ⌃

2. Give the workflow a name and make sure it is a SharePoint 2013 workflow.

Create List Workflow - Tasks   ?   ✕

Add a new workflow to your list

Enter a name and description for your new workflow

Name:

Notify About High Prio Tasks

Description:

Choose the platform to build your workflow on

Platform Type: SharePoint 2013 Workflow   ⌄

OK   Cancel

3. Click OK.

4. Set the end stage:

Stage: Stage 1

(Start typing or use the Insert group on the Ribbon.)

Transition to stage

(Insert go-to actions with conditions for transitioning to the stage)

5. Click on 'go to'.

6. Type "go".

7. Press Enter.

8. Select the stage 'End of Workflow'.

Transition to stage

Go to End of Workflow

9. Click on the Workflow settings button under the ribbon 'WORKFLOW' tab.

Workflow
Settings

10. Under Start Options, set the workflow to start automatically when an item is created:

Start Options

Change the start options for this workflow.

☑ Allow this workflow to be manually started

☑ Start workflow automatically when an item is created

☐ Start workflow automatically when an item is changed

➢ **Step 4, set the Conditions for the workflow**

1. In the Workflow settings page, click on the 'Edit workflow' link.

Use this page to view and manage settings for this workflow.

Workflow Information

Customization

Links to customization tools.

- ▣ Edit workflow ⟵
- ▣ Open associated list
- ▣ Open task list
- ▣ Open history list

2. Click on the 'Condition' button in the ribbon and select 'If any item equals value'.

Condition Action Stage Step Loop

Common Conditions

If any value equals value

3. This condition is now displayed in Stage 1.

Stage: Stage 1

If value equals value

4. Click on the first 'value' and set 'Current Item' to 'Priority'.

Stage: Stage 1

If   *fx*

(Sta   Define Workflow Lookup   ?   ✕

Transit   Field Data to Retrieve

(Inser   Choose the data source to perform the lookup on, then the field to
             retrieve data from:

             Data source: Current Item   ⌄

             Field from source: Priority   ⌄

             Return field as:

             Clear Lookup   OK   Cancel

5. Click OK.

6. Click on the second 'value' and select 'High'.

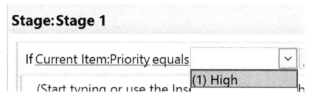

➤ **Step 5, create an Action for the workflow**

1. Click on the 'Action' button in the ribbon and select 'Send an Email'. This will add the text 'Email these users' to the stage.

2. Click on 'these users' in the stage.

3. Click on the lookup icon to the right of the 'To:' field.

4. Select 'Workflow Lookup for a User'.

5. Set the Current Item to get its value from the 'Assigned To' field.

6. Set the Return field to 'Email Addresses, Semicolon Delimited'.

7. Click OK to both dialogs, so that only the E-mail dialog remains.

➤ **Step 6, design the e-mail subject**

1. Write a text in the Subject field.

2. Click on the ellipsis button to the right of the subject field.

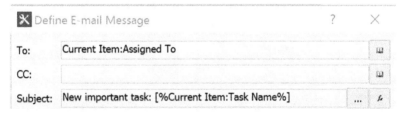

3. Click on 'Add or Change Lookup' at the bottom of the dialog that opens.

4. Set the Current Item to get its value from the 'Task Name' field.

5. Click OK to both dialogs so that only the e-mail dialog remains visible. Now the task name parameter has been added to the e-mail subject.

Define E-mail Message	?	✕
To:	Current Item:Assigned To	📖
CC:		📖
Subject:	New important task: [%Current Item:Task Name%]	... ƒ

> **Step 7, design the e-mail body**

1. Go to the Tasks list in **SharePoint** and create a new item.

2. Click on the ellipsis at the new item and open it in edit mode.

3. Copy the first part of the link to the task in edit mode. Exclude the part after ID=.

https://kdemo13.sharepoint.com/sites/DemoIntranet/sales/Lists/Tasks/EditForm.aspx?ID=

4. Enter your preferred text in the body field of the **SharePoint Designer** E-mail Message dialog.

5. Select the text you entered.

6. Click on the hyperlink icon to the right above the body field.

7. Click in the Address field of the dialog that opens.

8. Click on the ellipsis button to the right of the Address field.

9. Paste the ID link you copied from the task in edit mode into the new dialog that opens.

10. Make sure the cursor is placed after the link.

11. Click on the 'Add or Change Lookup' button at the bottom of the dialog.

12. Set the Current Item to get its value from the ID field.

13. Click OK. This adds the ID parameter to the task item URL.

![X] String Builder	?	✕

Name:

https://kalmstromnet.sharepoint.com/sites/kalmstrom.com-demos/Lists/tasks/EditForm.aspx?ID=[%
Current Item:ID%]

14. Click OK to both dialogs so that only the e-mail message remains visible.

15. Add any other information you prefer to the e-mail body.

16. Click OK.

> **Step 8, publish the workflow**

1. Click on the 'Check for Errors' button under the ribbon 'WORKFLOW' tab.

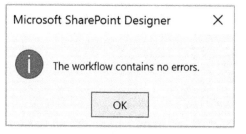

2. (Any errors will be marked with red. Correct them.)

3. Click OK to the dialog box when the workflow is error free.

Microsoft SharePoint Designer	✕
ⓘ The workflow contains no errors.	
OK	

4. Click on the 'Publish' button in under the ribbon 'WORKFLOW' tab.

> **Step 9, create a test task**

1. Go to the Tasks list in the **SharePoint** site.

2. Click on '+ new task'.

⊕ new task

3. Enter a task name, assign the task to yourself and set the priority to '(1) High'.

Task Name *	Test 2
Start Date	
Due Date	
Assigned To	Peter Kalmström x

Priority	(1) High ∨
Task Status	Not Started ∨

Save   Cancel

4. Click on 'Save'.

5. Go to your mailbox.

6. Check that the workflow has sent an e-mail with the correct task name in the subject.

7. Check that there is a link in the e-mail body.

Sweep   Move to ∨   Categories ∨ •••

New important task assigned to you: Test 2

Sales <no-reply@sharepointonline.com>
Today, 10:21 PM
Peter Kalmström ∀

Click here to edit the task

8. Check that the correct task opens in edit mode when you click on the link.

INSERT A VISIO WEB DRAWING INTO A VISIO

WEB ACCESS WEB PART

The Visio Web Access web part, which allows you to show live Visio drawings in SharePoint, is only available in the Enterprise subscriptions of Office 365. This web part can be used in wiki pages and web part pages, but it cannot be used in the new page model.

Before you start working with this exercise you need to create or download a Visio file. You can of course use any Visio drawing, but if you want to do the exercise with my file, you can download it from: http://www.kalmstrom.com/Tips/SharePoint-Online-Exercises/files/NetworkStore.vsdx

The Visio drawing is saved to a SharePoint document library as a Visio drawing, which is then added to a Visio Web Access web part in a new SharePoint wiki or web part page.

You can continue updating the Visio file that has been saved to SharePoint. The Visio Web Access web part will be updated each time you save your changes to SharePoint.

Goal

Show a Visio drawing in a Visio Web Access web part on a wiki page.

Actions

- Save the Visio drawing to a document library in the site where you want to add it
- Create a new wiki page
- Add a Visio Web Access web part to the new page
- Connect the web part to the Visio drawing
- Hide the web part crome

Demo:

http://www.kalmstrom.com/Tips/SharePoint-Online-Exercises/Add-Visio-Drawing-To-SharePoint.htm

> **Step 1, save a Visio drawing to SharePoint**

1. In **SharePoint**, right click on the SharePoint icon in the site where you want to add the Visio drawing and copy the URL.

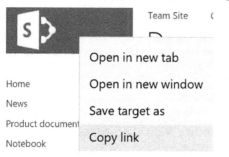

2. In **Visio**, open the file you want to add to SharePoint.

3. Open the 'File' tab.

4. Click on 'Save as'.

5. Click on the 'Browse' button.

6. Paste the URL you copied in step 1 above.

7. Select a document library in the site.

8. Save the drawing to the library as a Visio Drawing.

9. Click on 'Save'.

10. Check that the file has been uploaded to the **SharePoint** site document library.

> **Step 2, create a new wiki page**

1. Create a new wiki page in one of these two ways:

   a. If your site is using the classic experience interface, go to the home page of the site where you want to add the Visio drawing, click on the Settings gear in the right top navigation and select 'Add a page'.

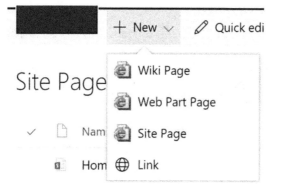

b. If your site is using the new experience interface, go to the Site Contents of the site where you want to add the Visio drawing and open the Site pages.

Site Pages   Wiki page library

Click on '+New' in the command bar and select 'Wiki Page'.

2. Give the new page a name and click on 'Create'.

3. The page opens in edit mode.

➢ **Step 3, add a Visio Web Access Web Part to the new page**

1. Open the 'INSERT' tab and click on 'Web Part'.

2. Select 'Business Data'.

3. Select 'Visio Web Access'.

4. Click on 'Add'.

> **Step 4, connect the Visio Web Access web part to the Visio drawing**

1. Click on the tool pane icon and select 'Edit Web Part'.

Visio Web Access

Select a Web Drawing

To display a Web Drawing in this web part, you mu Drawing.
To select a Web Drawing, open the tool pane, and URL web part setting.
Click here to open the tool pane.
How do I connect this web part to a Web Drawing

Minimize

Close

✕ Delete

Edit Web Part

Export...

This first time you edit the web part, you can also click on the link 'Click here to open the tool pane'.

2. Click on the ellipsis button to pick up the Web Drawing.

◀ Visio Web Access   ✕

⊟ Web Drawing Display

Web Drawing URL

[   ] [...]

3. Browse to the document library where you saved your Visio drawing and select it.

4. Click on 'Insert'.

5. Expand the "Appearance" section.

┌───┐
│ ◀ Visio Web Access   ✕ │
│ ⊟ Web Drawing Display   │
│   │
│   Web Drawing URL   │
│   ┌─────────────────────┐ ┌──────┐   │
│   │   │ │ ... │   │
│   └─────────────────────┘ └──────┘   │
│   ~~Force~~~~~~~nderin~~~~~~~~~W~~~   │
│ ⊟ Appearance   │
│   │
│   Title   │
│   ┌─────────────────────┐   │
│   │ Visio Web Access   │   │
│   └─────────────────────┘   │
│   │
│   Chrome Type   │
│   ┌──────────┐ ┌───┐   │
│   │ None   │ │ ∨ │   │
│   └──────────┘ └───┘   │
│ ⊞ Layout   │
│ ⊞ Advanced   │
│   ⌃ │
│   ┌──────┐ ┌────────┐ ┌────────┐   │
│   │ OK │ │ Cancel │ │ Apply │   │
│   └──────┘ └────────┘ └────────┘   │
└───┘

6. Set the 'Chrome Type' to None.

7. Click on OK at the bottom of the tool pane.

8. Click on 'SAVE' in the top right corner of the page.

ADD A LIVE CHART TO A PAGE

WITH EXCEL WEB ACCESS

The Excel Web Access web part, which allows you do show live Excel charts in SharePoint, is only available for the Office 365 E3 and E6 subscriptions.

When you have inserted the Excel chart in the web part on a SharePoint page, you can continue updating the Excel file in Excel Online or in the client version of Excel. If you just make changes in the chart, the Excel Web Access web part will be updated each time you save your changes. If you change the underlying data, you must also refresh the chart under the Analyze or Data tab.

In this exercise we are using an Excel file where the data is formatted as a table. The pivot table and chart is managed in a way that is suitable for the data in that file. The Excel chart is displayed in a SharePoint site called Sales.

Before you start working with this exercise you need to create or download an Excel file. You can use any Excel file, but if you want to do the exercise with my file, you can download it from:
http://www.kalmstrom.com/Tips/SharePoint-Online-Exercises/files/BicycleSales.xlsx

Refer to step 1 of the Connect App Parts exercise for instructions on how to format a range of Excel data as a table.

Format as
Table ▾

Goal

Add a live Excel chart in an Excel Web Access web part to the home page of the Sales department site.

Actions

- Open the Excel file and create a new pivot table
- Manipulate the pivot table to show how the total sales are distributed among products
- Create a chart from the new pivot-table
- Save the Excel spreadsheet to the Sales site document library
- Add a new Excel Web Access web part to the Sales home page
- Connect the web part to the Excel spreadsheet
- Edit the web part so that it looks as you prefer

Demo:

http://www.kalmstrom.com/Tips/SharePoint-Online-Exercises/Add-Chart-To-Excel-Web-Access.htm

➢ **Step 1, create an Excel pivot table**

1. Open the **Excel** file.

2. Open the ribbon 'Design' tab and click on 'Summarize with PivotTable'.

3. Click OK to the dialog box.

Create PivotTable dialog box:

- **Choose the data that you want to analyze**
  - ⦿ Select a table or range
    - Table/Range: Table1
  - ○ Use an external data source
    - Choose Connection...
    - Connection name:
    - ○ Use this workbook's Data Model
- **Choose where you want the PivotTable report to be placed**
  - ⦿ New Worksheet
  - ○ Existing Worksheet
    - Location:
- **Choose whether you want to analyze multiple tables**
  - ☐ Add this data to the Data Model

[OK] [Cancel]

4. In the Pivot Table Fields dialog, drag LineTotal to 'Values' and Branch to 'Rows'.

PivotTable F.. ▾   ✕

Choose fields to add to report: ⚙ ▾

| Search | 🔎 |

☑ **Branch**   ▲
☐ ProductCategory
☐ ProductName
☐ Color
☐ StandardCost
☐ ListPrice
☐ OrderQty
☑ **LineTotal**
☐ OrderDate   ▾

Drag fields between areas below:

▼ Filters	▐▌ Columns

▦ Rows	Σ Values
Branch ▾	Sum of Li... ▾

5. Edit the 'Sum of LineTotal' as you wish:

   a. Click on 'Sum of LineTotal' and enter a custom name in the Value Field Settings dialog.

   b. Click OK.

Sum of LineTotal

1	
99	
2	
18	
121	

Value Field Settings   ?   ✕

Source Name: LineTotal

Custom Name: Sum of LineTotal

Summarize Values By   Show Values As

Summarize value field by

Choose the type of calculation that you want to use to summarize data from the selected field

Sum
Count
Average
Max
Min
Product

[Number Format]   [OK]   [Cancel]

c. Open the ribbon 'Home' tab and edit the currency, number of decimals and other settings (or use the 'Number Format' button in the 'Value Field Settings' dialog).

Number

> **Step 2, create an Excel chart**

1. In the **Excel** pivot table worksheet, open the 'Analyze' tab and click on PivotChart.

Analyze	Design	♀ Tell me what you want to do				
Slicer			Clear ˅	*ƒx* Fields, Items, & Sets ˅		
Timeline			Select ˅	OLAP Tools ˅	PivotChart	Recommended
onnections	Refresh	Change Data Source ˅	Move PivotTable	Relationships		PivotTables
ter		Data	Actions	Calculations	Tools	

2. Select the chart option you prefer.

Insert Chart

All Charts

- ↰ Recent
- ▦ Templates
- ᴵᴵᴵ Column
- ⌁ Line
- ◔ Pie
- ☰ Bar
- 〰 Area
- ⁚⁚ X Y (Scatter)
- ᴵᴵᴵ Stock
- ⬡ Surface
- ⚹ Radar
- ⊞ Treemap

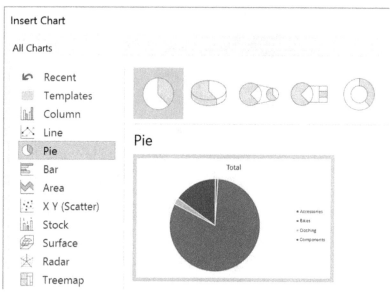

Pie

3. Edit the chart. For example:

a. Remove the explanations: select that part, right click and
   select Delete.

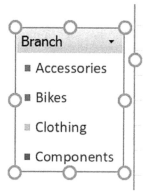

b. Click in the title and write a custom name.

c. Change the chart design under the ribbon 'Design' tab.

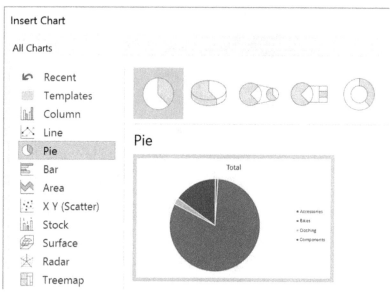

4. Note the chart name. It will be needed in step 5.

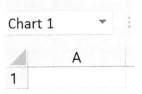

> **Step 3, save the spreadsheet to a SharePoint library**

1. In **SharePoint**, right click on the SharePoint icon in the site where you want to add the Excel chart and copy the URL.

S

Team Site

Open in new tab

Home

Open in new window

News

Save target as

Product document

Copy link

Notebook

2. Go to **Excel** and open the 'File' tab.

3. Click on 'Save as'.

4. Click on 'Browse'.

5. Paste the URL you copied in the address field.

6. (Remove the part "Forms/AllItems.aspx" from the URL.)

7. Log in, if necessary.

8. Save the Excel file in a document library.

Save As						×
↑	'ritukasp16/sites/ritukasp/Sales/Shared Documents	⌄	↻	Search Shared Documents		🔎
⭐ Quick access		S		Sales		
🖥 Desktop 📌				Documents		
⬇ Downloads 📌						
📄 Documents 📌	Type	Name		Modified By	Modified	
🖼 Pictures 📌						
Acess	📊	BicycleSales		Rituka	7/20/2016 10:49 AM	
images						

9. Go to the **SharePoint** site.

10. Open the document library and make sure that the Excel file is there.

> **Step 4, add the Excel Web Access web part to the homepage**

1. Go to the homepage of the **SharePoint** site where you want to add the chart.

2. Click on "EDIT" in the top right corner of the page.

   ☆ FOLLOW ✏ EDIT ⬚

3. Put the cursor where you want to place the Excel Web Access web part.

4. Open the ribbon 'Insert' tab and click on 'Web Part'.

5. Select 'Business Data' from the Categories

6. Select 'Excel Web Access' from the Parts.

7. Click on Add.

> **Step 5, connect the web part and the Excel spreadsheet**

1. Expand the tool pin accordion in the top right corner of the Excel Web Access web part and click on 'Edit Web Part'.

This first time you can also click on the tool pane link.

2. Workbook setting:

   a. Click on the ellipsis button and browse to the Excel file you saved to the documents library in step 3.

◄ Excel Web Access	✕

   Workbook Display

   Workbook:

   b. Click on 'Insert'.

   Select an Asset   ✕

   Current Location: Documents at http://ritukasp16/sites/ritukasp/Sales/Shared Documents

	All Documents ▾ Click to add new item		
☐ Content and Structure Reports	☐ Name	Modified	Modified By
☐ Contoso Content Types			
☐ Countries	📊 BicycleSales.xlsx ...	About an hour ago	Rituka
☐ Customers			
☐ Documents			
☐ Estonia			
☐ Form Templates			
☐ India			
▷ ☐ MicroFeed			
☐ Partners			
☐ Phone Messages			
☐ Reusable Content			

   Location (URL): /sites/ritukasp/Sales/Shared Documents   ✕   →

   Insert   Cancel

3. Type in the name of the chart noted earlier (Step 2, point 4) in the 'Named Item' dialog box in the tool pane.

....

Named Item:

| Chart 1| × | ... |

4. In the 'Type of Toolbar' dropdown, select 'None'.

Type of Toolbar:

None   ✔

5. Expand the 'Appearance' section.

6. Go to the 'Chrome type' dropdown and select 'None'.

⊟ Appearance

Title

Excel Web Access

...   .

Should the Web Part have a fixed height?
....

Chrome Type

None   ✔

⊞ Layout

⊞ Advanced

| OK | Cancel | Apply |

7. Click OK.

8. Click on 'Save' in the top right corner of the page.

☆ FOLLOW   🔗 SAVE   ⟭

CUSTOMIZE A MASTER PAGE FOOTER

In this exercise we will use SharePoint Designer 2013 to change the Master page so that a custom footer is added to all pages in a site, but not to dialogs. The method only works for the classic experience interface. The new page model does not use a master page, and when this is written there is no easy way to customize a page that has the new experience interface.

Note that generally neither Microsoft nor I recommend modifying the master page, but sometimes it is the only way to do things. Therefore I have decided to include this exercise in the book.

To install SharePoint Designer 2013, refer to the exercise Workflow that Sends E-mail Notifications about High Priority Tasks.

Goal

Customize a SharePoint .master page so that each page in the site displays a custom footer.

© Contoso Bicycles

Actions

- Open a SharePoint site in SharePoint Designer 2013
- Find the .master page that you want to customize, by default 'Seattle.master'
- Add the following .html code right before the end of the workspace PlaceHolderMain section:
  © Contoso Bicycles

The code above adds the text '© Contoso Bicycles' in white on a black background to the footer of all pages in the site. The class excludes dialogs, so dialogs will not have this footer.

Demo:

http://www.kalmstrom.com/Tips/SharePoint-Online-Exercises/Customize-Master-Page.htm

➢ **Step 1, open a .master page in SharePoint Designer 2013**

1. In the **SharePoint** site you want to customize, right click on the SharePoint icon and copy the URL to the site.

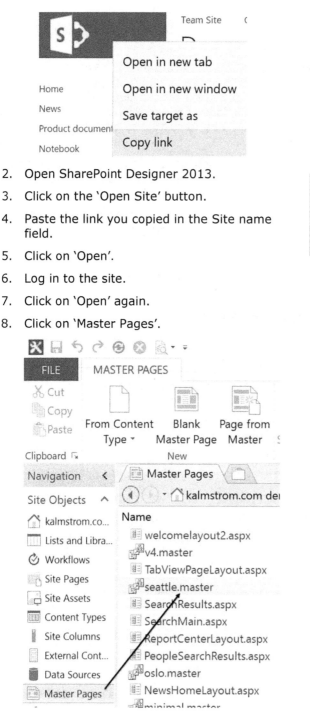

2. Open SharePoint Designer 2013.

3. Click on the 'Open Site' button.

4. Paste the link you copied in the Site name field.

Open Site

5. Click on 'Open'.

6. Log in to the site.

7. Click on 'Open' again.

8. Click on 'Master Pages'.

9. Select the .master page of the site, by default 'seattle.master'.

10. Click on 'Edit file' under 'Customization'.

Customization

Links to file customization tools.

▣ Edit file ⟵——————

▣ Manage all file properties in the browser

➢ Step 2, add .html code before the end of the body tag

1. Change the code '<div id= "Footer" class= "s4-notdlg" style= "background:black; color:white">© Contoso Bicycles</div>' so that colors and text suits your organization.

2. Use Ctrl+F to search for 'placeholdermain' in the current page.

```
        <asp:ContentPlaceHolder id="PlaceHolderMain" runat="server" />
    </SharePoint:AjaxDelta>
</div>
```

3. When you have found the place holder, copy the code that should be inserted.

4. Paste your .html code within the placeholder after the placeholder tag.

```
        <asp:ContentPlaceHolder id="PlaceHolderMain" runat="server" />
        <div id= "Footer" class= "s4-notdlg" style= "background:black; color:white">&copy; Contoso Bicycles</div>
    </SharePoint:AjaxDelta>
</div>
```

5. Click on 'Save'.

6. Select Yes to the warning.

➢ Step 3, test the footer

1. Go to the **SharePoint** site.

2. Refresh the page.

3. Check that the custom footer is displayed.

CREATE A PROJECTS DOCUMENT SET

When you work with projects within an organization, you often create a similar set of documents for each project, and templates are used to make the documents consistent. With a document set content type, you can have such documents created and named automatically when you create a new project item. By default the auto-created documents are named with the name of the project item + the name of the template.

When you create a new project item in a library that uses a document set content type, you will have the specified set of documents created automatically. The content writer can just open each document and start writing, instead of creating and naming several new documents.

All the documents for a project are found in one project item. In the library, each item will have the document set icon to show that it contains several files.

In this exercise we will create a document set content type that contains two files and has two custom columns.

Before you start this exercise, you need to prepare:

- Two documents that should be used in the document set

  - a Word file, here called "Project Specifications"

  - an Excel file, here called "Project Budget"

- An empty "Projects" library, to which you can add the new document set content type.

To have a consistent use of metadata, we will also create a term set for the project information in each file. This term set is created in the Term Store in the SharePoint admin center, so that it can be used by the whole organization.

Goal

Create a Projects Document Set content type with one Excel file and one Word file. The content type should have a Project Manager column and a Project Type managed metadata column tied to a Project term set in the Term Store.

Actions

- Create a new Managed Term Set called "Contoso Project Type" with the terms Merger, New Product, Product Enhancement and Administration
- Create a new content type inheriting from a Document Set called "Contoso Project"
- Add a Word document with the name "Project Specification" and an Excel file with the name "Project Budget" to the new content type
- Add a People & Group column with the name "Project Manager"
- Add a "Project Type" managed metadata column tied to the Managed Term Set "Contoso Project Type"
- Connect the "Contoso Project" content type to a document library and remove the default content type
- Add the custom site columns to the default library view
- Create three new projects:

  o "Titanium Mountain Bike"

  o "New Invoicing System"

  o "Better brakes on the Blue Lightning"

Demo:

http://www.kalmstrom.com/Tips/SharePoint-Online-Exercises/Document-Set-Content-Type.htm

➢ **Step 1, create a new Taxonomy Group with a new Term Set**

1. Open the App Launcher and click on the "Admin" button.

2. Select 'SharePoint' under 'Admin centers'.

3. Click on 'term store'.

SharePoint admin center

site collections	SEARCH
infopath	
user profiles	TAXONOMY TERM STORE
	English
bcs	◢ 🏠 Taxonomy ./2w8F+c5EEkkspwXCWYn/w==≋
term store	▷ 🗂 kalmstrom.com Solutions
	▷ 🗂 People

4. Under 'GENERAL' in the right pane, make yourself a Term store Administrator.

Term Store Administrators

You can enter user names, group names, or e-mail addresses. Separate them with semicolons. These users will be permitted to create new term set groups and assign users to the group manager role.

kate@kalmstrom.com;

5. Right click on the Taxonomy and select 'New Group'.

Taxonomy ./2w8F+c5EEkkspwXCWYn/w==≋

🗂 kalmstrom.com Solutions   New Group

6. Call the new group "Contoso".

7. Right click on the "Contoso Projects" group and select 'New Term Set'.

🗂 Contoso

🗐 New Term Set

8. Call the term set "Contoso Project Type".

9. Right Click on the "Contoso Project Type" term set and select 'Create Term'.

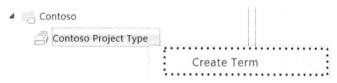

10. Enter the term "Merger".

11. Enter more terms:

   a. "New Product"

   b. "Product Enhancement"

   c. "Administration"

   - Contoso
     - Contoso Project Type
       - Merger
       - New Product
       - Administration
       - Product Enhancement

➤ Step 2, create a new Document Set Content Type

1. Click on the settings gear and select 'Site settings'.

2. Under 'Web Designer Galleries' click on 'Site content types'.

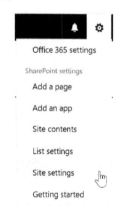

Office 365 settings

SharePoint settings

Add a page

Add an app

Site contents

List settings

Site settings

Getting started

Web Designer Galleries
Site columns
Site content types ←
Web parts
List templates

3. Click on the 'Create' link.

Site Settings ▸ Site Content Types

Create ←

4. Fill out the form.

    d. Name: Contoso Project.

    e. Parent Content Type: select from 'Document Set Content Types' and use the 'Document Set' content type.

Parent Content Type:

Select parent content type from:

| Document Set Content Types | ∨ |

Parent Content Type:

| Document Set ∨ |

Description:
Create a document set when you want to manage multiple documents as a single work product.

    f. Group: create a new group called "Contoso".

Put this site content type into:

○ Existing group:

| Custom Content Types | ∨ |

◉ New group:

| Contoso |

| OK | | Cancel |

    g. Click OK.

➤ **Step 3, add default content to the Document Set**

1. At Site Content Type >Contoso Projects, click on 'Document Set settings'.

Site Content Type Information

Name: Contoso Project

Description:

Parent: Document Set

Group: Contoso

Settings

- Name, description, and group
- Advanced settings
- Workflow settings
- Delete this site content type
- Information management policy settings
- Document Set settings ⟵━━━━━

2. Under 'Default Content', make sure that the Content Type 'Document' is selected and that the box for 'Add the name of the Document Set to each file name' is checked.

3. Click on 'Browse' and upload the Word file, "Contoso Project Specification", to the content type.

4. Click on 'Add new default content ...' and upload the Excel file, "Contoso Project Budget".

5. Click OK.

> **Step 4, add columns to the content type**

1. Create a **Project Manager** column.

   a. At Site Content Types >Contoso Project, click on the link 'Add from **new** site column'.

Columns

Name

Name

Title

- Add from existing site columns
- Add from new site column ◄───────
- Column order

b. Enter the name "Project Manager".

Column name:

| Project Manager| ✕ |

The type of information in this column is:

- ○ Single line of text
- ○ Multiple lines of text
- ○ Choice (menu to choose from)
- ○ Number (1, 1.0, 100)
- ○ Currency ($, ¥, €)
- ○ Date and Time
- ○ Lookup (information already on this site)
- ○ Yes/No (check box)
- ⦿ Person or Group

c. Select the radio button for 'Person or Group'.

d. Add the site column to the new group "Contoso".

Group

Specify a site column group.
Categorizing columns into groups will
make it easier for users to find them.

Put this site column into:

- ○ Existing group:

  | Base Columns ⌄ |

- ⦿ New group:

  | Contoso |

e. Select from where the person or groups should be chosen.

Choose from:

- ⦿ All Users
- ◯ SharePoint Group:

  Demo Intranet Members ∨

    f.   Click OK.

2. Add a "**Project Type**" column.

    a. At Site Content Types >Contoso Project, click on the link 'Add from **new** site columns'.

    b. Enter the name "Project Type".

Column name:

```
Project Type
```

The type of information in this column is:

- ◯ Single line of text
- ◯ Multiple lines of text
- ◯ Choice (menu to choose from)

- ◯ Summary Links data
- ◯ Rich media data for publishing
- ⦿ Managed Metadata

    c. Select the radio button for the column type 'Managed Metadata'.

    d. Add the column to the existing group "Contoso".

Put this site column into:

- ⦿ Existing group:

  ```
  Contoso                                  ∨
  ```
- ◯ New group:

    e. Select to use a managed term set and get metadata from the "Contoso Project Type" term set.

Enter one or more terms, separated by semicolons, and select Find to filter the options to only include those which contain the desired values.

After finding the term set that contains the list of values to display options for this column, click on a term to select the first level of the hierarchy to show in the column. All levels below the term you select will be seen when users choose a value.

◉ Use a managed term set:
Find term sets that include the following terms.

⊿ 🏠 Taxonomy_/2w8F+c5EEkkspwXCWYn/w==
    ⊿ 🏛 Contoso
        ⊿ 🗂 Contoso Project Type
             ⊙ Administration
             ⊙ Merger
             ⊙ New Product
             ⊙ Product Enhancement

    f.   Click OK.

➢ **Step 5, connect the Projects library to the new content type**

1. Open the "Projects" library.

2. Click on the settings gear and select 'Library settings'.

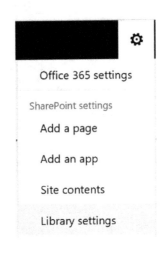

3. In the Library Settings, click on 'Advanced settings' under General Settings.

    General Settings

    ⬚ List name, description and navigation

    ⬚ Versioning settings

    ⬚ Advanced settings ⬅

Office 365 settings

SharePoint settings

Add a page

Add an app

Site contents

Library settings

4. Select 'Yes' to allow management of content types.

Settings › Advanced Settings

Content Types

Specify whether to allow the management of content types on this document library. Each content type will appear on the new button and can have a unique set of columns, workflows and other behaviors.

Allow management of content types?

⦿ Yes   ◯ No

5. Click OK.

6. In the new 'Content Types' group, click on 'Add from existing site content types'.

Content Types

This document library is configured to al

Content Type

Document

⬚ Add from existing site content types

7. Select the "Contoso" content types group.

Select site content types from:

Contoso ∨

Available Site Content Types:

Contoso Project

Content types to add:

Add >

8. Select the "Contoso Project" content type.

9. Click on Add.

10. Click OK.

➢ **Step 6, remove the default content type from the Projects library**

1. Click on 'Document' in the 'Content Types' section.

Content Types

This document library is configured to al

Content Type

Document

⬚ Add from existing site content types

2. Click on 'Delete this content type', so that only the "Contoso Project" content type is available for this library.

Settings

- Name and description
- Advanced settings
- Workflow settings
- Delete this content type
- Information management policy settings
- Document Information Panel settings

3. Click OK.

➢ **Step 7, add the custom site columns to the default view**

1. In the "Projects" library, click on the plus sign to the right of the columns and select 'Show/hide columns'.

+

Single line of text

Multiple lines of text

Number

Person

Date

More...

Show/hide columns

2. Check the boxes for the columns Project Manager and Project Type.

3. Use the arrows to set the appropriate column order.

4. Click on Apply at the top of the pane.

5. Open the View selector and select 'Save view'.

6. Keep the current name.

Save as   ✕

Save current view or type a new name

| All Documents | ✕ |

☑ Make this a public view

[Save]   Cancel

7. Click on 'Save'.

➢ Step 8, test the document set

1. Create a new project in the "Projects" library.

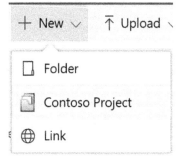

| + New ∨   ↑ Upload ⬎ |

☐ Folder

▣ Contoso Project

⊕ Link

2. Enter the name, "Titanium Mountain Bike".

3. Start writing the name of the responsible person and select the correct name among the choices.

Project Manager   Kate Kalmström x

Project Type   [   ] 🔗

4. Add a Project Type:

   a. Click on the icon to the right of the Project Type field.

   b. Select 'New Product' among the terms in the term set.

   c. Click on the 'Select' button.

   d. Click OK.

Select : Project Type   ✕

◢ 🖨 Contoso Project Type

  ⊙ Administration

  ⊙ Merger

  ⊙ New Product

  ⊙ Product Enhancement

Select >>	New Product

OK   Cancel

5. Click on the 'Save' button.

6. Check that the two files included in the document set have been properly named with the project name + the template name.

Projects › Titanium Mountain Bike

Titanium Mountain Bike

View All Properties
Edit Properties

⊕ New   ⬆ Upload   🔃 Sync   🔗 Share   More ∨

Find a file   🔎

✓	🗋	Name		Modified	Modified By
	🗏	Titanium Mountain Bike - Product Specification ⚏	•••	A few seconds ago	Kate Kalmström
✓	🗏	Titanium Mountain Bike - Project Budget ⚏	•••	A few seconds ago	Kate Kalmström

7. Click on 'Projects' to see the document set icon in the default library view.

Projects

✓	🗋	Name ∨
		Titanium Mountain Bike

➤ **Step 9, test by creating additional document projects**

1. Create the project "New Invoicing System" and select the Project Type 'Administration'.

2. Create the project "Better brakes on the blue lightning" and select the Project Type 'Product Enhancement'.

3. Check that the new projects have been created.

Projects

✓	🗋	Name ∨	Project Type ∨	Project Manager ∨
		Better lights on the blue lightning	Product Enhancement	Jitu Patidar
		New Invoicing System	Administration	Peter Kalmström
		Titanium Mountain Bike	New Product	Kate Kalmström

ABOUT THE AUTHOR

Peter Kalmstrom is the CEO and Systems Designer of the Swedish family business Kalmstrom Enterprises AB, well known for the software brand *kalmstrom.com Business Solutions*. Peter has 19 Microsoft certifications, among them several for SharePoint, and he is a certified Microsoft Trainer.

Peter begun developing his kalmstrom.com products around the turn of the millennium, but for a period of five years, after he had created *Skype for Outlook*, he also worked as a Skype product manager. In 2010 he left Skype, and since then he has been concentrating on his own company and on lecturing on advanced IT courses.

Peter has published two more books, *SharePoint Online from Scratch* and *Excel 2016 from Scratch*. Both are sold worldwide via Amazon. Next book will be *Office 365 from Scratch*.

As a preparation for lectures and books, Peter has created various video demonstrations, which are available on YouTube and at http://www.kalmstrom.com/Tips.

Peter divides his time between Sweden and Spain. He has three children, and apart from his keen interest in development and new technologies, he likes to sing and act. Peter is also a dedicated vegan and animal rights activist.

CPSIA information can be obtained
at www.ICGtesting.com
Printed in the USA
LVHW021049120619
620963LV00010B/241